SINCE
1854

MECHANICS' INSTITUTE

LIBRARY & CHESS ROOM

57 Post Street, San Francisco, CA 94104
(415) 393-0101

HONG KONG PRECINCTS

A curated guide to the
city's best shops, eateries,
bars and other hangouts

HONG KONG PRECINCTS

A curated guide to the
city's best shops, eateries,
bars and other hangouts

PENNY WATSON

hardie grant publishing

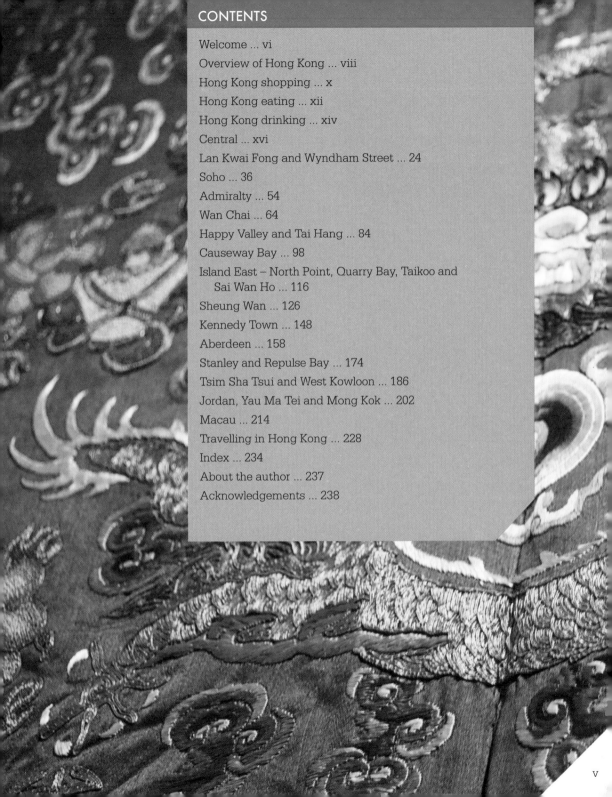

CONTENTS

WELCOME

Welcome to *Hong Kong Precincts*. In a city that changes, in the blink of an eye, this book is my humble attempt at capturing a snapshot of the best eating, drinking and shopping venues in 15 precincts across the city.

It's a timely tome. In the past few years, the Hong Kong food scene has been turned on its head, becoming truly international and offering world-class cuisine in the form of some very funky-arse restaurants. Drinking venues have followed suit, with once rare options – like rooftop and alfresco bars – becoming part of the cocktail landscape. The coffee scene has also found its feet. Cool cafes – non-existent five years ago – can now be found in the most out-of-the-way places, usually with an antipodean barista at the helm. Similarly, artisan shops and boutiques offer an alternative to the big brands that have for so long been the hallmark of the city's shopping scene.

Happily, this is only one side of Hong Kong. To really getting to know a city you must sidestep the comforts and familiarities of home and go local. In each chapter, I've tried to include at least one Chinese restaurant, market or 'mom and pop' shop (as the noodle shops are known), where you can happily slurp on a bowl of noodles sitting next to a local.

Get out and about. Hong Kong's red taxis are as iconic to this city as black cabs are in London. They're cheap and readily available. On Hong Kong Island, the lovely old double-decker trams are the city's own form of slow transport. The open-air Star Ferries provide a glimpse of days gone by; don't go home without taking one across Victoria Harbour. Further afield, the MTR system (one of the best in the world) and bus network can get you to the far reaches of Hong Kong Island, Kowloon and the New Territories. The ferry system puts the dozens of islands – and Macau – within reach. Alternatively, walk. My favourite Hong Kong haunts have been found on foot.

No book would be big enough to incorporate all the greats, but hopefully my inclusions – and tips from locals featured in each chapter – will guide you to streets, neighbourhoods and precincts where you will find your own gems.

Penny Watson

TSING YI

GUANGDONG

CHINA

HONG KONG, SAR

MACAU, SAR

SOUTH CHINA SEA

LANTAU ISLAND

PENG CHAU

GUANGDONG

PENINSULA DE MACAU

MACAU

MACAU
214

ILHA DE TAIPA

HEI LING CHAU

HENGQUIN DAO

ILHA DE COLOANE

SOUTH CHINA SEA

TO
MACAU
(SEE INSET MAPS
ABOVE RIGHT)

CHEUNG CHAU

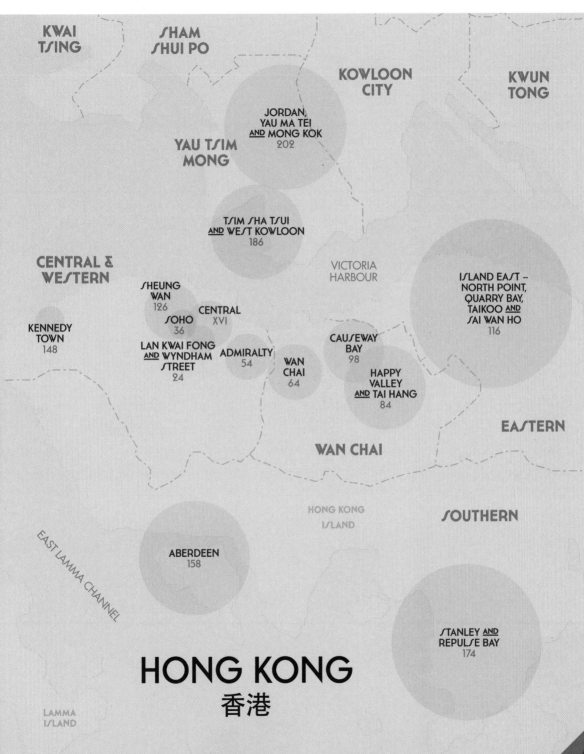

KWAI TSING

SHAM SHUI PO

KOWLOON CITY

KWUN TONG

JORDAN, YAU MA TEI AND MONG KOK
202

YAU TSIM MONG

TSIM SHA TSUI AND WEST KOWLOON
186

VICTORIA HARBOUR

ISLAND EAST –
NORTH POINT, QUARRY BAY, TAIKOO AND SAI WAN HO
116

CENTRAL & WESTERN

SHEUNG WAN
126

CENTRAL
XVI

SOHO
36

KENNEDY TOWN
148

LAN KWAI FONG AND WYNDHAM STREET
24

ADMIRALTY
54

WAN CHAI
64

CAUSEWAY BAY
98

HAPPY VALLEY AND TAI HANG
84

EASTERN

WAN CHAI

HONG KONG ISLAND

SOUTHERN

ABERDEEN
158

EAST LAMMA CHANNEL

STANLEY AND REPULSE BAY
174

HONG KONG
香港

LAMMA ISLAND

Lucky cat

Bamboo steamer

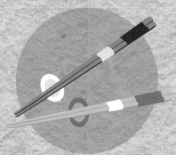

Chopsticks

Ceramic umbrella holder

Bespoke shoes

Birdcage

Handbags galore
(fake or authentic)

Antique snuff bottle
(used to hold powdered tobacco)

Cheong sam dress

Fu dog statue
(placed at front doors to keep evil spirits away)

Anything from Shanghai Tang (i.e. umbrella, pen, plate)

Jade bangle

Panda eye mask

Tailored suit

Blue and white ceramics

Hand-carved wooden mooncake moulds

Traditional tea set

Mao statue

Fish congee
(rice porridge)

Roasted goose

Mooncake

Zha liang
(rice noodle roll with fried dough)

Wonton and fish ball soup

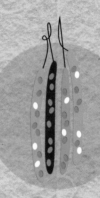

Laap cheung
(Chinese sausage)

Curry fish balls

Dan tart
(Portuguese egg tart)

Cheung fan
(rice noodle roll)

Siu mai
(pork dumplings)

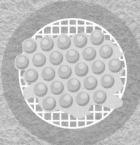

Egg waffle
(sweet waffles made from
egg batter)

Spicy crab

Cha siu bao
(pork bun)

Chicken feet

Pineapple bun

Siu yuk
(roasted suckling pig)

Xia long bao
(soup dumpling)

Fresh abalone

Chinese tea

Yuanyang coffee-tea drink

Hong Kong beer

Baijiu
(white distilled spirit)

Typhoon Eastern
Lightning beer

Hot herbal teas

Sour plum drink
(also called suan mei tang)

Bubble tea

Tsingtao

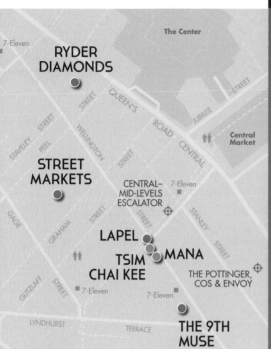

Hong Kong's CBD, on the north shore of Hong Kong Island, is one of the world's most eye-catching. Wedged between the steep jungle slopes of Victoria Peak mountain and the shores of Victoria Harbour, its teetering, shiny, glass-and-metal edifices lend a futuristic air to the city, an effect that's pronounced at night when the skyline glitters like a galaxy of stars.

At street level, old gardens, churches and heritage buildings survive from British colonial times. Aromatic shrines dot the sloping streets. Market vendors sell live seafood, hundred-year-old eggs and antiquities. Against this backdrop is the modern Hongkonger: well-dressed, hardworking and just as easily won over by a bowl of cheap noodles (*see* Tsim Chai Kee p. 014) as a Gucci bag.

Central Station;
Hong Kong Station

CENTRAL

24   JUN 8OT6

SHOP
1 STREET MARKETS
2 JOYCE
3 LAPEL
4 PEDDER BUILDING
5 SHANGHAI TANG
6 RYDER DIAMONDS
7 VICKIE'S SHOES
8 THE 9TH MUSE

SHOP, EAT AND DRINK
9 IFC MALL
EAT
10 MANA
11 TSIM CHAI KEE

1.

STREET MARKETS
Peel, Graham and Gage sts,
Central
Open Mon–Sun 6am–8pm

Flapping fish, tubs of tofu and mountains of mushrooms: not far from the city's flashiest retail district is an open-air food market that has operated since 1841. Despite government attempts to move them indoors, about 130 fixed-pitch hawkers still ply their trade here, contributing to the vibrant street life that Hong Kong is known for. Graham Street's narrow pathway is covered by awnings and lined with stalls selling fruit and vegetables, homemade noodles and so-called '100-year-old' eggs. Polystyrene boxes brim with fish and crustaceans on neighbouring Gage Street, and on Peel Street rice sellers, traditional medicine stores and repair shops jostle for space next to hip cafes and restaurants.

JOYCE

New World Tower,
16–18 Queens Rd, Central
2810 1120
www.joyce.com
Open Mon–Sun
10.30am–7.30pm

Forty years ago, Joyce was the first store to showcase international designers – a big step in redefining fashion for the colony. Fast-forward to today and this chic, split-level boutique is still leading the field with fashion collections housed in exquisite surrounds that include art exhibitions and installations. It's a fine-label-lover's paradise. Pick up a fitted raincoat by French designer Wanda Nylon, a summer suit by China's Xander Zhou or a scarf from New York's Title of Work. Delve into the shelves for expensive beauty products, including Renouve hand lotion, Francis Kurkdjian perfume or, intriguingly, dragon-blood eye-lifting pads by Wei. A doorman at the entrance sets the scene for this lavish experience.

3.

LAPEL
98 Wellington St, Central
2851 1969
www.tailorlapel.com.hk
Open Mon–Sun 10am–8pm

It can be slightly baffling finding a tailor in Hong Kong, given they all look like carbon copies of each other. Reality check – a lot of the clothes are made in the same factory over the border in China. Armed with this information, look no further than Lapel, a friendly mob who will happily measure you up for a stylish classic work shirt or hand-stitched suit and have it back to you almost overnight. Failing that, they'll ship it home and keep your measurements on file for reordering. If you have a favourite shirt that fits to perfection, take it with you and they'll replicate it with exactitude times ten or 20. The walls are lined with pinstripes and checks in Italian and English fabrics to keep you looking good nine to five.

PEDDER BUILDING
12 Pedder St, Central
Open Mon–Sun 10am–6.30pm

- -

Sitting narrowly on Pedder Street, surrounded by modernity, this charming eight-level heritage building with a colonnaded arched facade is one of Hong Kong's elderly darlings. Once the home of Shanghai Tang (*see* p. 006), it now hosts **Abercrombie & Fitch** on the ground level. Upstairs, there are upmarket galleries such as contemporary **Gagosian**, and Chinese art specialists **Pearl Lam** and **Hanart TZ Gallery**. Other truly good finds here include **The Lavish Attic**, a luxury men's accessories boutique; **Burgundy etc**, a cellar devoted to the famed region; and **Red Chamber Cigar Divan**, a smoking lounge owned by Sir David Tang (founder of Shanghai Tang), with wood-carved furniture, antique artwork and 300 Havana cigars to puff on.

5.
SHANGHAI TANG
1 Duddell St, Central
2525 7333
www.shanghaitang.com
Open Mon–Sun 10.30am–8pm

Born and bred in Hong Kong, this global boutique for high-end Chinese-inspired luxury should top your list of retail must-dos. Rents skyrocketed at the original Pedder Street building, so owner Sir David Tang restyled the brand's flagship store with this newer, more glam, four-storey version. Oodles of space, grand ceilings, immaculate staff and the signature ginger lily scent pervade so that the place oozes wealth and sophistication. If your budget allows a splurge, this is the spot for tasteful gifts and souvenirs, the ones you'll want to keep forever: colourful cheongsam Chinese-style dresses, tailored suits, horoscope cufflinks, jewellery boxes, silver-plated chopsticks and beautiful pens. Duddell's (*see* p. 016) is on the top two floors.

6.
RYDER DIAMONDS
Level 10, Kimley Building,
142–146 Queens Rd, Central
2805 2589
www.ryderdiamonds.com
Open Mon–Fri 10am–6.30pm
(Sat by appointment)

The bling is big in Hong Kong. This diamond studio, covering two floors of an old Central building, is the go-to place for anyone looking for diamond engagement rings, wedding bands, earrings and bracelets. Step into the nondescript elevator on a side street and out into a classy black-and-white showroom. There are beautiful pieces on display, but it's best to take advantage of the bespoke service. With founder Sally Ryder (*see* p. 022) at the helm, Ryder Diamonds does everything by hand, from sketching designs, picking the diamonds and crafting the pieces. It's a rare craft in the world of mass production and machine-made jewellery.

7.
VICKIE'S SHOES
6 Li Yuen St East, Central
2522 9013
Open Mon–Sat 10.30am–8pm,
Sun 11am–7pm

Faux croc, fake snake, pleather or leather: if it's cheap, made-to-order shoes you're after then this everyday shop in a market side street is the place to park your peds. Vickie's has a great reputation for its 'interpretation' of designer styles and ability to fit them to any foot, big or small (up to size 44 in women's shoes). Choose a style from the shapes and sizes lining the walls, then take a load off while looking through swatch books for colours and materials. Heel heights and trimmings can also be customised. Shoes cost between HK$300 and HK$700 and can be picked up within a couple of weeks, or sent home – a reliable service I've taken advantage of (and postage is cheap in Hong Kong).

HOT TIP
About 2 kilometres south-west of Hong Kong Island, Lamma Island is a fun daytrip, with tiny villages, seafood restaurants, beaches and walks. Ferries to Yung Shue Wan, the main settlement on Lamma, depart from Central Ferry Pier 4.

8.

THE 9TH MUSE

Level 12, One Lyndhurst Tower,
1 Lyndhurst Tce, Central
2537 7598
www.the9thmuse.com
Open Mon–Sun
10.30am–7.30pm

High-school roommates and
long-time friends Charlotte
Hwang and Jing Zhang
opened this devilishly dishy
accessories boutique after
discovering beautiful and
eclectic pieces on their
travels. Countries represented
include Korea, Cambodia and
Namibia. They stock cutting-
edge (and reasonably priced)
rings and necklaces, vintage
bags, funky sunglasses,
scarves, elegant stationery
and headily aromatic
perfumes. You can also
pick up unique homewares,
such as sugar bowls, hand-
printed greeting cards and
woven baskets. Many of
the designers are relative
unknowns, so expect to find
one-off items. Keep your
eyes peeled as it's obscurely
located in an office block, not
a shopping mall, which is part
of the fun.

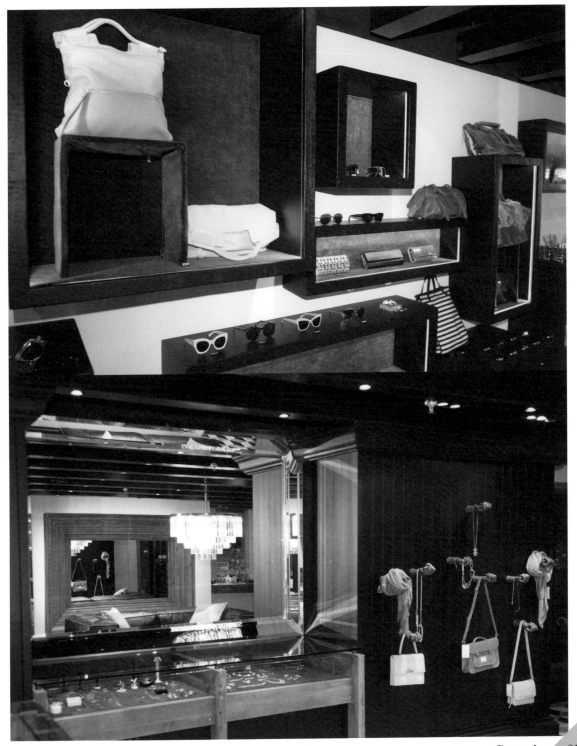

9.

IFC MALL

8 Finance St, Central
2295 3308
www.ifc.com.hk
Open Mon–Sun 10am–10pm
(most shops)

Heartbeat of the Hong Kong banking world, fashionable grand-daddy of shopping malls, go-to place for a good feed: IFC can be all things to all people. This 88-storey building, visible from much of the city (and only pipped in the height stakes by ICC; *see* p. 189) could be a day's outing in itself. You can spend a pretty penny here with brands like **Chanel**, **Kate Spade**, **Jimmy Choo** and **Claudie Pierlot**. Achingly cool **Lane Crawford** is a *very* Hong Kong department store. Restaurants include Michelin-starred **Lei Garden** and office-worker eateries such as **Panino Giusto**. **Fuel Espresso** has A1 coffee. **Isola**, a long-lunch Italian brasserie, has a balcony with cross-harbour Kowloon views. Rooftop **Red Bar** can kickstart any evening with dance tunes and cocktails.

10.

MANA

92 Wellington St, Central
2851 1611
www.mana.hk
Open Mon–Sun 10am–10pm

Far from its hippie origins, organic produce has become the busy Hongkonger's guarantee of fresh quality food – particularly important in a region where food scandals often make headlines. Organic Mana cafe specialises in 'flats', rounds of unleavened bread, freshly baked in a brick oven, sprinkled with Mana's own zaatar (thyme, sumac, sesame seeds and sea salt) then topped with various ingredients. The delightful Mana Bliss comes with avocado, hummus, cucumber and salad, or go for haloumi burgers, salads and mezze platters. The flats are made from organic flours and there's a gluten-free option. Other ingredients are sourced from the owners' local organic farms.

11.

TSIM CHAI KEE

98 Wellington St, Central
2850 6471
Open Mon–Sun 9am–10pm

This end of Wellington Street has a reputation for old-school noodle and dumpling joints, all of them cheap and cheerful and with the kind of retro decor we love. While Tsim Chai Kee has opted for clean lines and a more contemporary look, it still serves up kick-butt won tons and has earned itself a Michelin recommendation for its effort. It buzzes at lunchtime. Orders are taken from punters lined up outside who are then ushered onto share tables as stools become available. There's a basic menu with an English translation, but you can't go wrong ordering soup with pork dumplings, fish balls and yellow noodles (HK$27). Top it with potent chilli sauce and get a side of garlicky steamed greens. Curiously, it's BYO napkin.

12.

DUDDELL'S

Levels 3 & 4, Shanghai Tang
Building, 1 Duddell St, Central
2525 9191
www.duddells.co
Open Mon–Sun 12pm–1am

Secreted away atop Shanghai
Tang (*see* p. 006), this two-
level Cantonese restaurant
is a shrine to exquisite taste.
On the lower level, the hush-
hush dining room in yellow
and white hues delivers
hifalutin meals to an up-
market lunch crowd; dishes
include pan-fried crab claw
with caviar, and fried beef
cube with wasabi and soy
sauce. Abalone and bird's
nest dishes also feature, a
nod to tradition.

Upstairs it is like stepping
into a (very wealthy) friend's
salon and library. There's a
mix of designer chairs and
couches, and an art collection
curated by artists themselves,
including Ai Weiwei. Dim sum
can be eaten ever so politely
with teas called Joyous
Moment and Hearty Pleasure.
Outside, a huge garden deck
with pot plants and bamboo
furniture sits pretty amid the
skyscrapers. It's the perfect
place for a margarita made
with Chinese five-spice,
vanilla tequila, fennel seed,
triple sec and grapefruit.

LUPA & LA TERRAZZA

Level 3, LHT Tower,
31 Queens Rd, Central
2796 6500
www.luparestaurant.com
Open Mon–Sun 12–3pm &
6–11pm

Look for the Gap store, then look up. The little balcony you see is an inner-city secret, one of the few places where you can enjoy Italian nosh the way the Italians like it – alfresco. Lupa is a large restaurant in the Roman osteria style, a smart business-lunch place with a reputation for excellent antipasto – cured hams and salamis, pickled vegetables, tomato and green salads, olives and breads. À la carte specialities include braised oxtail and celery-root ravioli, and veal saltimbocca served with breaded green beans and balsamic vinegar. At the rear of the restaurant La Terrazza is one of the best outdoor bars in the city. It has 40 wines by the glass, covering every region of Italy. On Sundays there's brunch and jazz (from 12pm to 3pm).

14.

MOTT 32
Basement, Standard Chartered
Building, 4–4A Des Voeux Rd,
Central
2885 8688
www.mott32.com
Open Mon–Sun
11.30am–3pm & 6pm–12am

Named after the famed
Chinese convenience store
on 32 Mott Street in New
York, this flash Cantonese
restaurant in an old bank vault
was extravagantly designed
by Joyce Wang (*see* p. 062).
Wang successfully married
the industrial elements of
New York with echoes of
classic Chinese iconography –
wall paintings, calligraphy
brushes and lampshades. It
is one of the few Cantonese
restaurants with a farm-to-
table philosophy and it shows
in the dim sum. Specialities
include quail egg and black
truffle dumplings (which
should be eaten as soon as
they come to the table so the
quail egg doesn't overcook)
and char sui (barbecued pork).
Deviating from Cantonese
slightly is the lovely and
delicate apple-wood Peking
duck. Cocktails have a local
touch, none more so than
the Milk Tram (vodka, vanilla
syrup, almond milk, green tea,
egg white and cinnamon).

SEVVA

Level 25, Prince's Building,
10 Chater Rd, Central
2537 1388
www.sevva.hk
Open Mon–Sat 12pm–late

- -

It was supposed to be pronounced 'savour', but the wordplay never caught on. Fortunately, guests at this devil-may-care moneyed establishment are too busy ogling the harbour views to worry. This is where Hongkongers come to show off: expats bring their parents, wealthy Chinese bring their families and cashed-up bankers bring their dates. The rest of us can pull up a pew and marvel at the excess. Couches, throw cushions and amber glowing lights make life comfortable outdoors. Inside scrubs up like a *Vogue* interior with a green vertical garden, floor-to-ceiling windows, leather poufs and decadent fabrics. The fare is a combination of influences. Order small plates of sushi and sashimi or mini foie-gras burgers. Make sure you heed the dress code: 'easy glam'.

16.

ZUMA

Levels 5 & 6, Landmark,
15 Queens Rd, Central
3657 6388
www.zumarestaurant.com
Restaurant open Mon–Thurs
11.30am–2.30pm & 6–11pm,
Fri 11.30am–2.30pm &
6–11.30pm, Sat 11am–1pm,
2–4pm & 6–11.30pm,
Sun 11am–1pm, 2–4pm &
6.30–11pm; bar open
Mon–Wed 11.30am–1.30am,
Thurs–Fri 11.30am–2am,
Sat 5pm–2am

Start an evening at Zuma
bar with a Tokyo Rose, a
rose-infused Tanqueray gin,
Campari and Martini Rosso
cocktail. Somehow it pairs
brilliantly with the nu-disco
tunes, leather seating, dark-
wood-hued furniture and
luminous walls of this popular
after-five bar. Accessed via
a swanky spiral staircase,
the adjoining Japanese
restaurant downstairs has a
full-length open kitchen where
various workstations create
authentic modern izakaya,
sushi, sashimi and robata
(charcoal grill) dishes. Tartare
of salmon, yellowtail rolls and
spicy beef tenderloin with
sesame, red chilli and sweet
soy should start you off nicely.
The tasting menu paired with
hot sake is a trip down the
road to culinary excellence.
The weekend buffet brunch,
where you can try everything,
is *the* best in Hong Kong.

Sally Ryder came to Hong Kong from Australia more than a decade ago. With big support from local industry she founded Ryder Diamonds (*see* p. 008), a grassroots business that creates bespoke diamond jewellery.

Where do you like to eat lunch in Central?

For something upmarket, Gaia is fantastic; I love the ambience of the piazza. For lunch at my desk, Noodlemi and K-Roll, both just down the road from our office, are cheap and cheerful.

What are your favourite Hong Kong drinking venues?

I'm a creature of habit, and usually meet the girls on a Friday night at Wagyu (*see* p. 031). Those guys sure know how to look after their regulars!

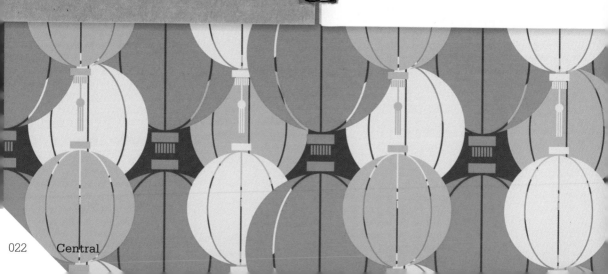

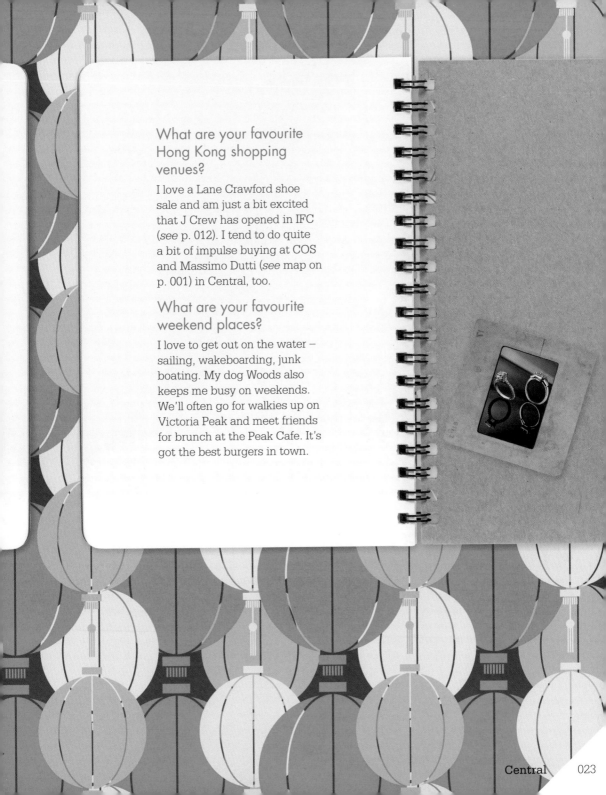

What are your favourite Hong Kong shopping venues?

I love a Lane Crawford shoe sale and am just a bit excited that J Crew has opened in IFC (*see* p. 012). I tend to do quite a bit of impulse buying at COS and Massimo Dutti (*see* map on p. 001) in Central, too.

What are your favourite weekend places?

I love to get out on the water – sailing, wakeboarding, junk boating. My dog Woods also keeps me busy on weekends. We'll often go for walkies up on Victoria Peak and meet friends for brunch at the Peak Cafe. It's got the best burgers in town.

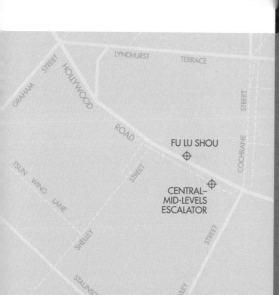

Talk to anyone who has partied in Hong Kong and they'll tell you they either passed through Lan Kwai Fong (LKF) or passed out in it. This small grid of streets in Central on Hong Kong Island, spilling down the lee side of Hollywood Road to Queens Road, has long been party central. Streets are blocked off festival-style at night and revellers get lubricated with lethal jelly shots from stalwart Al's Diner.

More recently the party has moved – or rather spread – south to Wyndham Street, a continuation of Hollywood Road that turns north down the hill. This area is considered a little more sophisticated than LKF, with more wine bars than pubs, but both areas have party-hardy restaurants.

Central Station

LAN KWAI FONG AND WYNDHAM STREET

SHOP

1 TERESA COLEMAN TIBETAN GALLERY
2 JOHANNA HO

EAT AND DRINK

3 BRICKHOUSE
4 FISH & MEAT
5 FRINGE CLUB
6 WAGYU

DRINK

7 LE BOUDOIR

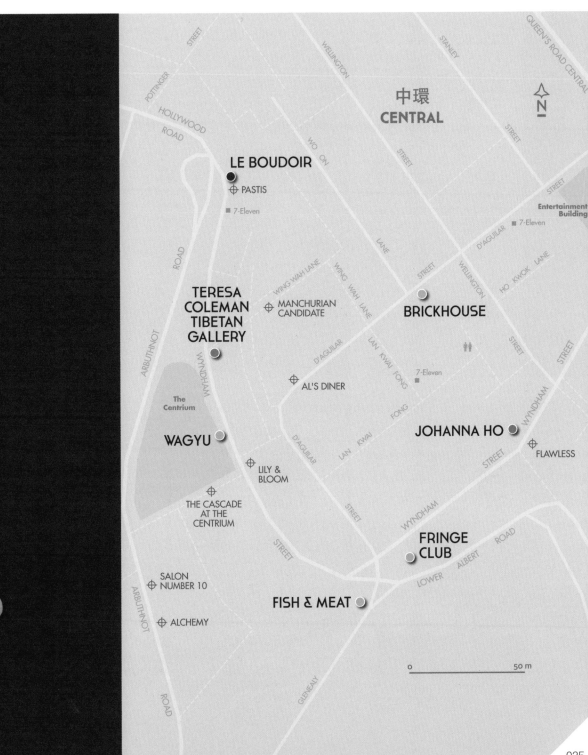

中環
CENTRAL

N

LE BOUDOIR
⊕ PASTIS

■ 7-Eleven

Entertainment
Building
■ 7-Eleven

TERESA
COLEMAN
TIBETAN
GALLERY

◆ MANCHURIAN
CANDIDATE

BRICKHOUSE

◆ AL'S DINER

7-Eleven
■

The
Centrium

WAGYU

JOHANNA HO

⊕ FLAWLESS

⊕ LILY &
BLOOM

⊕ THE CASCADE
AT THE
CENTRIUM

FRINGE
CLUB

⊕ SALON
NUMBER 10

⊕ ALCHEMY

FISH & MEAT

0   50 m

1.

TERESA COLEMAN TIBETAN GALLERY

55 Wyndham St, Central
2526 2450
www.teresacoleman.com
Open Mon–Sun 9.30am–7pm

Hollywood Road, Hong Kong's very first commercial strip, remains home to the city's antique (and faux antique) shops and boutiques, most of them at the Sheung Wan end. This one, where Hollywood meets Wyndham Street, is a favourite. Teresa Coleman, a Brit, has been sourcing the mainland continent's most elegant old wares for more than 20 years. Among the vases, Tibetan rugs, statues, jewellery and furniture are her speciality – rare chi fu, the silk-woven dragon robes worn by ministers to the Chinese imperial court. In this elegantly curated shop-cum-gallery, you can admire the chi fu, and pick up smaller, less expensive items, such as calligraphy brushes, rings and ornate boxes. Serious buyers can book an appointment to go upstairs to **Teresa Coleman Fine Arts** for more expensive treasures.

JOHANNA HO

13 Wyndham St, Central
2722 6776
www.johannaho.com
Open Mon–Sun 11am–8pm

Fashion designer Johanna Ho is Hong Kong–born, UK-trained. While her label has featured on catwalks from New York to Tokyo, her fashionable finery feels best purchased at her flagship store on home soil. On the steep steps of Wyndham Street, this is one of a cluster of boutiques appealing to fashionistas with coin to spare. Ho is queen of experimenting with different knit techniques and textures and combining them with structured designs. Some of her stuff is a little lacy, but goods of desire include triangular trousers in luscious pinks, draped-sleeve tops that sit just right and knitted pullovers with detailing that sets them apart from other labels.

3.

BRICKHOUSE

20A D'Aguilar St (via Brick La),
Lan Kwai Fong, Central
www.brickhouse.com.hk
Open Mon–Wed 6pm–2am,
Thurs–Sat 6pm–4am

That bag stall. Yes, that one with the cheap Louis Vuittons. Slip through it into a little lane that hides one of Hong Kong's coolest urban Mexican joints. Brickhouse takes most people by surprise. The graffiti-covered walls, pumping tunes, mostly male staff (who look like they're out of a skate ad) and covert location that screams 'find me' work to sensational effect. There are no bookings, so pull up a seat at the bar first for a diabla (jalapeño vodka, raspberries, pomegranate and lemon) and a stick of corn (covered in chilli mayonnaise, lime, grated cheese and coriander). When a table comes up, order the likes of rib-eye tacos with crispy manchego cheese, grilled tomato salsa and coriander, beet fries with Cajun mayonnaise, watermelon salad, market fish ceviche … get my drift?

4.

FISH & MEAT

Levels 1 & 2, 32 Wyndham St,
Central
2565 6788
www.fishandmeat.hk
Open Mon–Sun 12–11pm

Homemade Sicilian lemonade with blueberry jam and thyme should kick off lunch nicely. If you're feeling feisty, add vodka and prosecco. Like the name suggests, this stylish farm-to-table eatery with Scandinavian influences is all about pairing back the culinary layers so that the raw ingredients please the palate, be it the Devon crab in the endive, avocado and jalapeño salad, or the artichoke in the truffle risotto. This is a feat given the lengthy menu. The industrial space, with low-slung ceilings, concrete floors and exposed plumbing has been softened with reclaimed wooden tables and doors, jam-jar pendant lights and 'Scandinavian farmhouse' tools of trade – a meat slicer, leather aprons, an old chisel. Grab a table outside for a view over to the Fringe Club (*see* p. 030). Entry is via steep Glenealy Street.

3.

4.

HOT TIP
Need a facial? A pedi?
A massage? Flawless
(www.flawless.hk.com) on
Wyndham Street ticks all
the boxes. You can even
buy Havaianas if you have
forgotten your flip-flops.

5.

FRINGE CLUB
2 Lower Albert Rd, Central
2521 7251
www.hkfringe.com.hk
Open Mon–Sun 12pm–late

On the corner of Wyndham Street and Lower Albert Road, the Fringe Club is an arty epicentre where theatre, dance, photography, art, music and comedy take centre stage. The stucco-and-brick heritage building, an old dairy-farm depot, has studios, ongoing exhibitions and theatres that host Cantonese drama and gigs such as the best of the Melbourne Comedy Festival. There's a cafe on the hillside with couches, art catalogues and lattes. For buffet lunches or a beer, head upstairs to a massive underutilised open-air beer garden. The Fringe, bless it, is hopelessly average at marketing itself, so drop in to get the lowdown.

6.

WAGYU
Unit 3, Centrium Building,
60 Wyndham St, Central
2525 8805
www.casteloconcepts.com
Open Mon–Sun 8am–late

It might be the smallest bar on this sociable stretch of Wyndham Street, but Wagyu remains a firm favourite with the locals who take up increasingly large chunks of sidewalk as the day draws on. The bar began as a holding pen for thirsty diners about to be seated at the spiffy adjoining Australian-owned restaurant (eggs Benedict, steak sandwiches, excellent flat whites all day), but it has held its own as a post-work starting place for expats planning a big night out. Free canapés and antipodean wines by the glass are other enticements at this hangout for homesick Australians.

7.

LE BOUDOIR

Basement, 65 Wyndham St,
Central
2530 3870
www.french-creations.com/
boudoir
Open Mon–Sun 6pm–3am

There's more than a hint of
Parisian burlesque at this
sumptuous crimson-tinted
bar found down a red-velvet-
lined staircase next to sister
establishment **Pastis** (*see*
map on p. 025). The cosy
basement location adds a
hint of counterculture and
the predominantly French
accents complete the picture.
There's a long polished bar
with chandeliers overhead
where you can sip on a glass
of Belgian Duvel or Dutch
Karmeliet beer. Or settle into a
Victorian-era sofa, surrounded
by gilt-edged mirrors and
frames, for a cocktail. Try the
Courtisane with kiwi fruit,
mint, champagne and apple
vodka, or a Porn-Star Martini
with vanilla vodka, honey,
lime, passionfruit and a shot
of bubbles on the side. Catch
the two-hour dance-troupe
show at 10pm on the last
Tuesday of every month.

Eddie McDougall was born in Hong Kong but hails from the beautiful King River wine region in Victoria, Australia. When Hong Kong's wine taxes were abolished in 2009, he returned to Hong Kong and started the Flying Winemaker. This LKF wine shop and bar has been ahead of the curve in the local wine market and spawned a local television show, exploring wine and Asian cuisine.

What is Hong Kong's relationship to wine?

Hong Kong is wine crazy! With so many festivals, tastings, events, parties, dinners and winemakers passing through, it has truly become a wine lover's mecca, surpassing places like London and New York. But it will take a hit at some point – speedy growth can reflect short-sighted players.

What was the last great wine you drank?

A Castello y Gaye 1936 Reserva. I drank this at a snobby wine dinner I was invited to by some friends at Crown Wine Cellars, in Shouson Hill. I was in heaven!

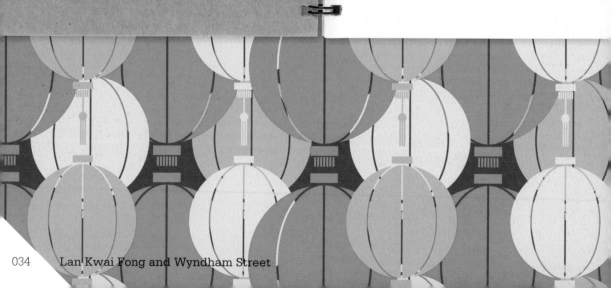

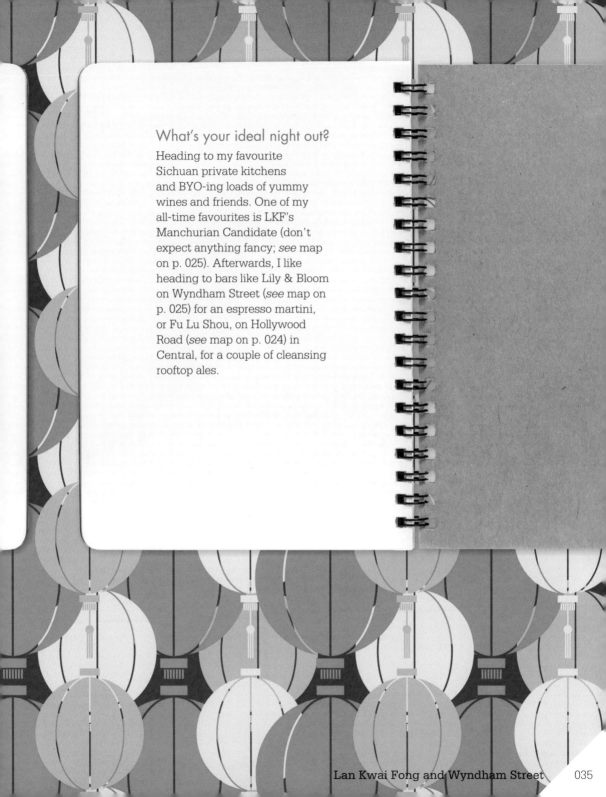

What's your ideal night out?

Heading to my favourite
Sichuan private kitchens
and BYO-ing loads of yummy
wines and friends. One of my
all-time favourites is LKF's
Manchurian Candidate (don't
expect anything fancy; *see* map
on p. 025). Afterwards, I like
heading to bars like Lily & Bloom
on Wyndham Street (*see* map on
p. 025) for an espresso martini,
or Fu Lu Shou, on Hollywood
Road (*see* map on p. 024) in
Central, for a couple of cleansing
rooftop ales.

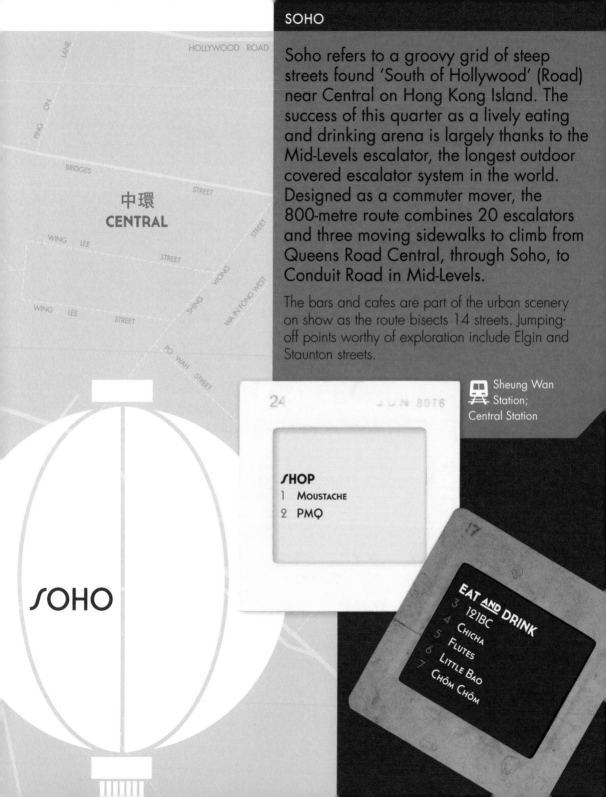

SOHO

Soho refers to a groovy grid of steep streets found 'South of Hollywood' (Road) near Central on Hong Kong Island. The success of this quarter as a lively eating and drinking arena is largely thanks to the Mid-Levels escalator, the longest outdoor covered escalator system in the world. Designed as a commuter mover, the 800-metre route combines 20 escalators and three moving sidewalks to climb from Queens Road Central, through Soho, to Conduit Road in Mid-Levels.

The bars and cafes are part of the urban scenery on show as the route bisects 14 streets. Jumping-off points worthy of exploration include Elgin and Staunton streets.

Sheung Wan Station; Central Station

SHOP

1 MOUSTACHE
2 PMQ

EAT AND DRINK

3 121BC
4 CHICHA
5 FLUTES
6 LITTLE BAO
7 CHÔM CHÔM

HOLLYWOOD ROAD

LANE

PING ON

BRIDGES

STREET

中環
CENTRAL

WING LEE
STREET
STREET

WING LEE STREET

SHING WONG STREET

WA IN FONG WEST

PO WAH STREET

24   JUN 8916

17

SOHO

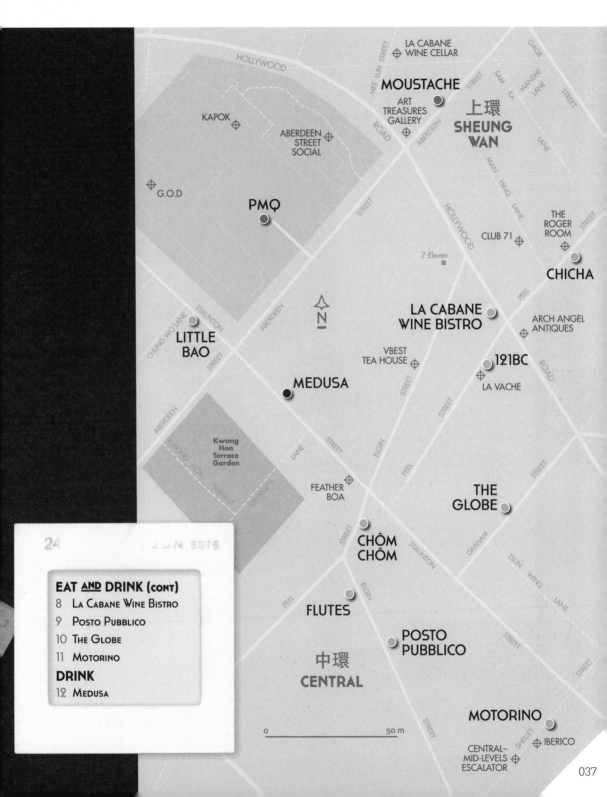

HOLLYWOOD

LA CABANE
WINE CELLAR

MEE LUN STREET

MOUSTACHE

ART
TREASURES
GALLERY

上環
SHEUNG
WAN

KAPOK

ABERDEEN
STREET
SOCIAL

ROAD

ABERDEEN

SAM KA STREET

MANSHE LANE

GAGE

STREET

LANE

G.O.D

PMQ

STREET

HOLLYWOOD

MAN HING LANE

CLUB 71

7-Eleven

THE
ROGER
ROOM

CHICHA

PEEL

STAUNTON

LITTLE
BAO

CHUNG WO LANE

ABERDEEN

STREET

N

LA CABANE
WINE BISTRO

ARCH ANGEL
ANTIQUES

VBEST
TEA HOUSE

121BC

LA VACHE

ROAD

MEDUSA

STREET

STREET

ABERDEEN

Kwong
Hon
Terrace
Garden

KWONG HON

TERRACE

GEORGE'S

LANE

STREET

ELGIN

PEEL

THE
GLOBE

STREET

GRAHAM

STREET

TSUN WING LANE

FEATHER
BOA

CHÔM
CHÔM

STAUNTON

24   JUN 8076

EAT <u>AND</u> DRINK (CONT)
8   LA CABANE WINE BISTRO
9   POSTO PUBBLICO
10 THE GLOBE
11 MOTORINO
DRINK
12 MEDUSA

PEEL

STREET

ELGIN

FLUTES

中環
CENTRAL

POSTO
PUBBLICO

STREET

STREET

MOTORINO

IBERICO

0   50 m

CENTRAL–
MID-LEVELS
ESCALATOR

SHELLEY

STREET

037

1.

MOUSTACHE

31 Aberdeen St, Soho
2541 1955
http://moustachehongkong.com
Open Tues–Sat 11.30am–7pm
(Mon by appointment)

In San Francisco they have
Al's Attire, in Melbourne
it's Captains of Industry, in
Hong Kong it's Moustache.
Dapper duo Alex Daye and
Ellis Kreuger opened their
bespoke tailor shop in 2009
with a mission to deliver high-
quality, hand-stitched suits
made from the finest fabrics –
tropical-weight and worsted
wools, cottons, linen and silk
blends. Their house-cut suit
is an homage to Hong Kong in
the 1960s (think Tony Leung
in one of my favourite movies,
In the Mood for Love), or
choose from bespoke dolphin-
print bathing shorts, paisley-
lined country blazers, piped
pyjamas, silk dressing gowns
and denim Bermuda shorts.
The store itself is a living room
of loveliness with eclectic
prints and pictures colouring
the walls, an oversized mirror
and a lounging canine on the
floor. Try on a fedora or buy
a luxurious Hong Kong–map
handkerchief.

PMQ

35 Aberdeen St, Soho
2870 2335
www.pmq.org.hk
Open Mon–Sun 7am–11pm

Rarely do local creative types enjoy as much hype as when this heritage-listed building reopened in 2014. Built in 1951 as the Police Married Quarters, the overbearing, U-shaped, eight-storey, double-block building is typical of postwar modern architecture: functional with nought to endear it bar porthole windows. But it has been redone well. What it lacks in looks it makes up for in soul with 100 or so shops – many of them start-ups – selling everything from jewellery, metalwork and art to homewares, fashion and footwear. It's particularly good for home-grown design shops like Kapok (*see* p. 066) and G.O.D. (*see* p. 176).

3.

121BC

42–44 Peel St, Soho
2395 0200
www.121BC.com.hk
Open Tues–Sat 5.30pm–late

Little Italian osteria-cum-enotecas with genuine European character are not so easy to come by in Hong Kong. Gorgeous 121BC, sitting contentedly next to the neon-lit French restaurant **La Vache**, is therefore the pick of this up-and-coming Peel Street pocket. Old steel-framed windows offer outsiders a view of the cosy-but-contemporary interior and it's a good look: a glitzy chandelier lights a long wooden share table and stools line a bar brimming with Italian wine and twinkling wine glasses. The fare is to share, and changes daily with seasonal availability: grilled asparagus with soft polenta, rosemary and reggiano cheese; potato ravioli with tomatoes, anchovies and olives. The sommelier, Simone, is excellent, recommending unique Italian drops.

4.

CHICHA

26 Peel St, Soho
9637 7701
www.conceptcreations.hk
Open Mon–Sun 12–3pm &
6–11pm

Memories of eating guinea pig in Peru be gone! Chicha is proof that South American cuisine, an amalgamation of Spanish, Japanese and Andean influences, is alive and kicking. Extending in three tiers along Peel Street, this lively eatery has a bar atmosphere; it's especially spirited when the house is full. There's a dining room with staid wood-panelled walls, downlights and bench seats or join the animated after-work crowd on stools around an open kitchen. Fish tacos with rocoto (a type of pepper/capsicum) aioli are the house speciality or go for a trio of ceviche. The wine list is entirely South American or you can buy Peru's famed Inca Kola. The restaurant also gets points for having no service charge.

3.

4.

HOT TIP
Have a drink at the
Caribbean-themed
bar the Roger Room at
39 Peel Street and order
Peruvian snacks from sister
establishment Chicha (*see*
opposite page) across
the road.

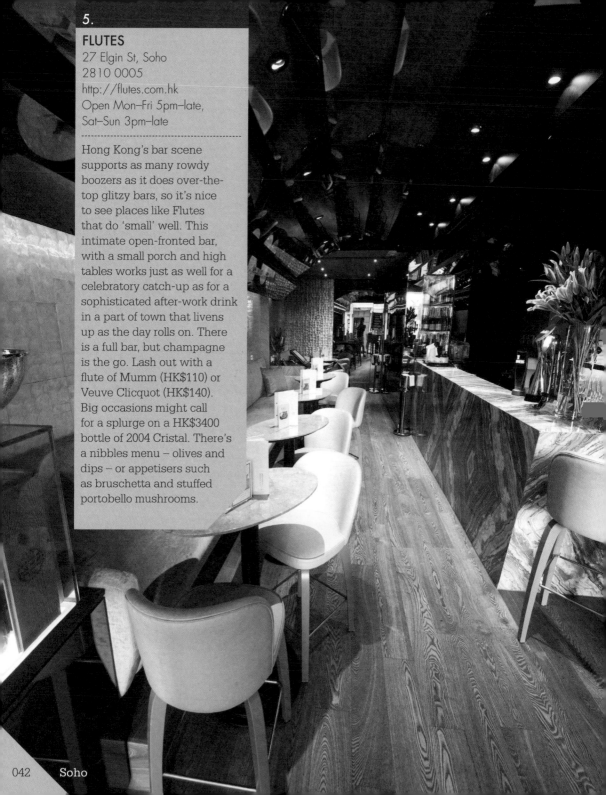

5.

FLUTES

27 Elgin St, Soho
2810 0005
http://flutes.com.hk
Open Mon–Fri 5pm–late,
Sat–Sun 3pm–late

Hong Kong's bar scene supports as many rowdy boozers as it does over-the-top glitzy bars, so it's nice to see places like Flutes that do 'small' well. This intimate open-fronted bar, with a small porch and high tables works just as well for a celebratory catch-up as for a sophisticated after-work drink in a part of town that livens up as the day rolls on. There is a full bar, but champagne is the go. Lash out with a flute of Mumm (HK$110) or Veuve Clicquot (HK$140). Big occasions might call for a splurge on a HK$3400 bottle of 2004 Cristal. There's a nibbles menu – olives and dips – or appetisers such as bruschetta and stuffed portobello mushrooms.

LITTLE BAO

66 Staunton St, Soho
2194 0202
www.little-bao.com
Open Mon–Sat 6–11pm

- -

Little Bao first raised its head at Island East Markets (*see* p. 118) and from little things big things grew. This cracking Chinese-fusion eatery, with its cutesy, neon-pink, cartoon mascot, may be tiny, but the offerings and nightly queue are big. The eponymous little bao is a fluffy white bun stuffed with various fillings, including sweet-soy-braised pork belly with pickled leek and cucumber. Other delectable fusion dishes nod to Japanese and Korean ingredients and include pan-fried short-rib dumplings, steamed Venus clams, and Little Bao fries with roasted-tomato sambal, Kewpie mayonnaise and coriander. The teeny drinks list includes eight craft beers, a sake, two cocktails and a refreshing pomegranate hibiscus iced tea. For dessert? Ice-cream sandwich.

7.

CHÔM CHÔM

58–60 Peel St, Soho
2810 0850
www.chomchom.hk
Open Mon–Tues 6pm–late,
Wed–Sun 4pm–late

Vietnam's bia hoi (fresh beer) street eating culture has been given the Soho makeover here, with French cooking techniques adding that extra *je ne sais quoi*. Chef Peter Cuong Franklin has taken a sleek cafe-cum-bar interior and added Vietnamese art, ceiling fans and industrial metal windows for a casual-but-classy dining experience. Sit on the front porch for street eating or smell the heady telltale mix of garlic, coriander and chilli in the dining room with open kitchen. Specialities from the charcoal grill include cha ca Hanoi, which is Vietnamese sole fillet cooked with brown butter, turmeric, shallots, spring onion and fresh dill. The cocktails are on theme: try the Thai-basil-flavoured Pho-jito or a Hanoi 75 laced with gin. Or simply roll with a Saigon beer.

LA CABANE WINE BISTRO

62 Hollywood Rd, Soho
2776 6070
http://lacabane.hk
Open Mon–Sat 12pm–late

What La Cabane lacks in space, it more than makes up for in oh-so-French character. The wooded theme outside, complete with bar for street drinking, continues indoors, where exposed bricks, timber-paling walls, a swing chair suspended from the ceiling and wine-barrel tables take you out of Hong Kong and into the cellar doors of France. The wines here are from small organic vineyards that favour natural processes, so are rare and eclectic in a down-to-earth way. Pair a wine, champagne or cider by the glass with pork terrine, beef tartare or fried frogs' legs. Or opt for a fromage platter that might include roquefort or comté. The bistro's sister, **Wine Cellar** (*see* map on p. 037), is at 97 Hollywood.

9.
POSTO PUBBLICO
28 Elgin St, Soho
2577 7160
www.postopubblico.com
Open Mon–Sun 11.30am–late

Hats off to PP. Before this slice of Italy opened in the heart of Soho, Hongkongers were hard-pressed knowing what an heirloom tomato was, let alone fresh mozzarella (the curd of which is flown in by a family friend in New York City). The restaurant also scored foodie points when it became one of the first to source fresh natural ingredients from parent company Homegrown's organic farm in the New Territories. With exposed brick walls, dark bentwood chairs and an open kitchen, this is a bustling osteria, a bar-cum-casual-diner where an antipasti platter and bowl of pasta (cappelletti nonna Francesca, for example – ravioli filled with chicken, pesto and ricotta) go down as well as a chilled glass of prosecco.

10.
THE GLOBE
45–53 Graham St, Soho
2543 1941
http://theglobe.com.hk
Open Mon–Sun 10am–2am

If you're looking for a good homey English gastropub, erm … you're in the wrong country. Except, perhaps for the Globe. This spacious Hong Kong stalwart hidden behind a small entry on Graham Street is the closest you'll get. The publican Toby Cooper has a penchant for suds, selling more than 100 craft bottled beers and – at last count – nine tap beers. There are stools around a central bar and comfy couches in the 'living room' (which has books, games and a plasma screen for films and sport). Otherwise, nab a booth or a table for some quality pub grub: roast guinea fowl, pulled lamb shanks, posh fish and chips. Try the Typhoon Eastern Lightning beer made at a brewery on Lantau Island.

9.

9.

10.

11.

MOTORINO
14 Shelley St, Soho
2801 6881
www.motorinopizza.com
Open Mon–Sun 12pm–12am

The surprise package here is the signature dish – a brussels-sprout pizza. 'What the … ?', I hear you say. 'That's a culinary travesty!' Don't decry it till you try it, I say. Motorino hails from Brooklyn so the fit-out is old-style New York with striped walls, bench seats and tiled dados. It's casual, but smart. The menu favours speciality cured meats and strong earthy cheeses like pecorino, but it's also keen on using 'disappeared ingredients', which brings us back to brussels sprouts. Still not convinced? Then order the soppressata pizza topped with fior di latte cheese, spicy salami, fresh chillies and garlic, and one of three Italian wines by the glass. The staff plug in their own tunes here so you can expect a happy medley of random music.

12.

MEDUSA
Basement, 49 Staunton St, Soho
2858 3129
www.facebook.com/bar.
medusa.hk
Open Mon–Sun 6pm–1am

Ok, so here's the deal. **Feather Boa** (*see* map on p. 037) is a lavish bar with an interior like something out of *Moulin Rouge*. It's awesome – but only if you can get in. Enter Medusa, a more welcoming underground joint that makes you feel like you're drinking Prohibition-style in Caravaggio surrounds. The fruit (strawberry, mango, watermelon and lychee) daiquiris made from seasonal market produce are so potent you'll forget your surname. Australian expat owners Philip and Carmen have also invented dessert cocktails like the best-selling Two Girl Guides in a Tent, a secret mix of five liqueurs topped with toasted marshmallow. Catch live flamenco on Wednesdays, jazz and blues trombone on Thursdays. Happy hour is 6pm until 8pm.

Frenchman Arnault Castel moved to Hong Kong after being inspired by Wong Kar-wai's *Chungking Express*. In the 19 years since his move, Arnault founded Kapok (*see* p. 066), with its focus on designers, quality craftsmanship and creativity. At last count, there were 11 variations of this lifestyle store, including a 'crafted in Hong Kong' version at PMQ (*see* p. 039).

What is your favourite Hong Kong neighbourhood?

I like the Star Street neighbourhood in Wan Chai (*see* p. 064) where we have one of our Kapok stores (*see* p. 066). There's a great terrace in front of the store surrounded by trees and with no cars – which is really rare in Hong Kong. What struck me about this neighbourhood is that it sometimes feels very Chinese, sometimes very European – the perfect fit for a Hong Kong store started by a French guy. It's close to everything, but has a little bit of a quiet, 'lost in time' feeling.

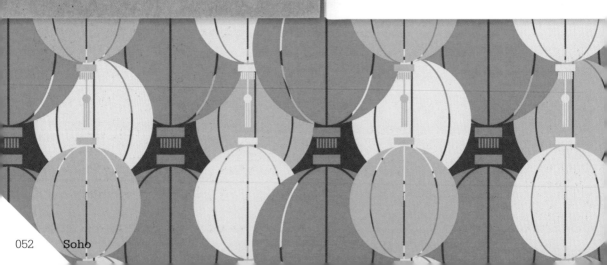

Who are your favourite local designers?

Teddyfish (Hong Kong/France) has simple hand-painted canvas bags that are like artworks. I also like Void Watches, launched in Hong Kong as the single vision of Swedish designer David Ericsson of Square Street (*see* p. 132). Void has a unique take on watch design, using simple yet expressive shapes that give the watches an almost architectural expression. Another favourite is So...Soap!, which commits to local production and trains soap makers, supporting them in community-based initiatives.

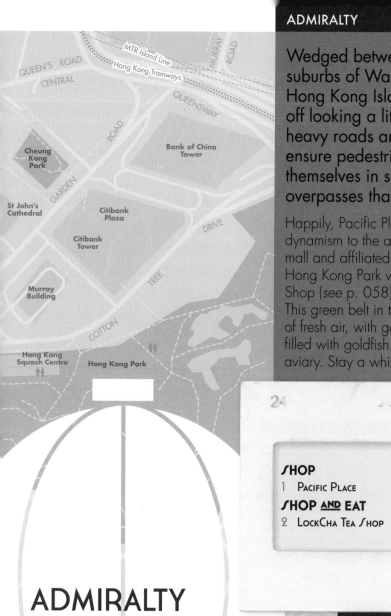

ADMIRALTY

Wedged between the extroverted suburbs of Wan Chai and Central on Hong Kong Island, Admiralty can come off looking a little dull. Its wide traffic-heavy roads and faceless office buildings ensure pedestrians are more likely to find themselves in shopping malls and on overpasses than on colourful streets.

Happily, Pacific Place (see p. 056) lends some dynamism to the area, with its excellent shopping mall and affiliated high-end hotels. Then there's Hong Kong Park where you'll find LockCha Tea Shop (see p. 058) and the Museum of Tea Ware. This green belt in the middle of the city is a breath of fresh air, with gardens and waterfalls, ponds filled with goldfish and terrapins, and a huge aviary. Stay a while.

Admiralty Station

SHOP
1 PACIFIC PLACE

SHOP AND EAT
2 LOCKCHA TEA SHOP

EAT AND DRINK
3 AMMO
4 CAFÉ GRAY DELUXE

Map labels

QUEEN'S ROAD CENTRAL
MTR Island Line
Hong Kong Tramways
QUEENSWAY
MURRAY ROAD
GARDEN ROAD
Bank of China Tower
Cheung Kong Park
St John's Cathedral
Citibank Plaza
Citibank Tower
DRIVE
TREE
Murray Building
COTTON
Hong Kong Squash Centre
Hong Kong Park

ADMIRALTY

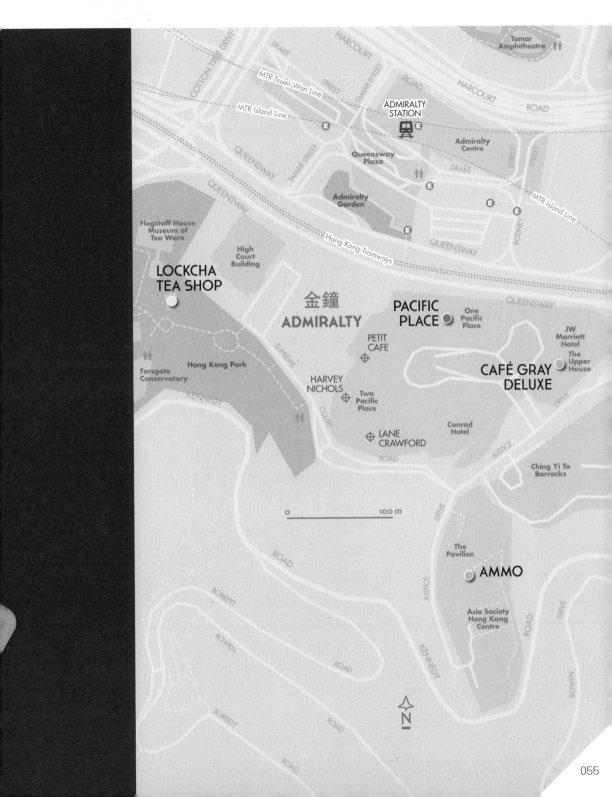

1.

PACIFIC PLACE

88 Queensway, Admiralty
2844 8900
www.pacificplace.com.hk
Open Mon–Sun 10am–12pm

Rarely do shopping malls look this good. Surrounded by flash hotels (including the Upper House; *see* p. 060) and three office towers, Pacific Place oozes contemporary luxury with unifying natural wood, stone and bronze design features. It feels more like a flash department store than a mall. But mall it is with a cinema, restaurants and a veritable feast of global fashion brands, including **Bottega Veneta**, **Chloé**, **Coach**, **Marc Jacobs**, **Miu Miu**, **Ted Baker** and **Vilebrequin**. For the local equivalent, check out Hong Kong label **Vivienne Tam**. Shanghai Tang (*see* p. 006), Joyce (*see* p. 003) and chic department stores **Harvey Nichols** and **Lane Crawford** make it a one-stop shopaholic's dream. On level four, **Petit Café**, with outdoor seating, serves up pastries, sandwiches and espresso coffee in lovely floral paper cups.

HOT TIP

After exploring Hong Kong Park follow the signs over Garden Road to Hong Kong Zoo, a similarly green oasis. More garden than zoo, it has marvellous birdlife, monkeys and serene places to sit.

2.

LOCKCHA TEA SHOP

K.S. Lo Gallery, Cotton Tree Dr,
Hong Kong Park, Admiralty
2801 7177

www.lockcha.com
Open Mon–Fri 10am–8pm,
Sat–Sun 10am–9pm; closed
every second Tues of the month

Tucked away amid the
greenery and birdsong of
Hong Kong Park, this
quaint shop in a grandiose
colonial building is part
speciality boutique, part
teahouse. Carved wooden
shelves hold tea wares –
scoops, pots, cups and
canisters – all with distinctive
Chinese ornamentation.
The tea comes direct from
mainland tea farms and
thus is unblended, pure,
single-harvest tea, which is
a good thing, especially as
it's not factory processed.
Sit down for an informal
tea ceremony with the
learned staff or try traditional
(uniquely vegetarian) dim
sum served amid a decor of
carved-wood wall panels and
calligraphy paintings.

3.

AMMO

Asia Society Hong Kong Center,
9 Justice Dr, Admiralty
2537 9888
www.ammo.com.hk
Open 12pm–12am

Housed in what was once
a British army explosives
compound, Ammo is the
drinking hub of Hong
Kong's legal set. It sits in
the lush green grounds of
the brilliantly cultural Asia
Society, where various
historical buildings have been
given seductive makeovers.
This one combines high
ceilings and military motifs
with extravagant spiral
chandeliers and copper
embellishments so shiny the
room sparkles. Despite the
opulence, it's actually quite
a relaxed place to dine, with
a Euro-centric menu leaning
towards Italian and French –
ravioli stuffed with zucchini,
buffalo mozzarella with red
prawns, pan-seared scallops
with foie gras. There is also
high tea on offer and British-
army-approved cocktails such
as the English Garden, a mix
of Hendrick's gin, elderflower
liqueur, cucumber, mint
and lime.

4.

CAFÉ GRAY DELUXE

Level 49, The Upper House,
Pacific Place, 88 Queensway,
Admiralty
3968 1106
www.cafegrayhk.com
Restaurant open Mon–Sun
6.30–10.30am, 12–2.30pm,
3.30–5.30pm & 6–10.30pm;
bar open Mon–Sun 11am–1am

Sitting in the clouds on the
top of Hong Kong's most
salubrious boutique hotel,
the **Upper House**, Café Gray
has movie-set status. It's
somewhere George Clooney
would sit sipping a cocktail
with the city lights twinkling
in the background. With
a European menu, wines
from little-known vineyards
(one on east coast USA, for
example) and impeccable
staff, it is perhaps a tad
pretentious, but with views
of Hong Kong Park, Victoria
Harbour and the hilly peaks
beyond Tsim Sha Tsui, it
remains popular. Try Thai
basil duck consommé and
ginger dumplings for brunch,
and black-truffle-steamed
seabass for dinner. Catch
sunset in the bar with a Hong
Kong Highball in hand.

MEET THE HONGKONGER
JOYCE WANG
INTERIOR DESIGNER

After winning a commission to renovate the cabana rooms in the iconic Hollywood Roosevelt Hotel in Los Angeles, Joyce Wang returned to hometown Hong Kong and went on to design Ammo (*see* p. 060) and later Mott 32 (*see* p. 018).

How do you define Hong Kong's restaurant style?

We're seeing interesting concepts from independent operators, and bigger groups like Maximal Concepts (which owns Mott 32) and the people behind Yardbird (*see* p. 145). Restaurants are moving closer to becoming holistic 'lifestyle concepts'. Casual, street-culture dining is huge, with places like Chôm Chôm (*see* p. 044) and Chachawan (*see* p. 142) popping up all over the city! Restaurants are also moving to exciting, gentrified areas like Sai Ying Pun, Tai Hang and Kennedy Town, where I'm a big fan of Sunday's Grocery (*see* p. 154).

Where do you find inspiration?

My inspiration comes from film and music and from spending time with people who engross themselves in these mediums. I also draw inspiration from my travels. I'm a big foodie so whenever I'm abroad,

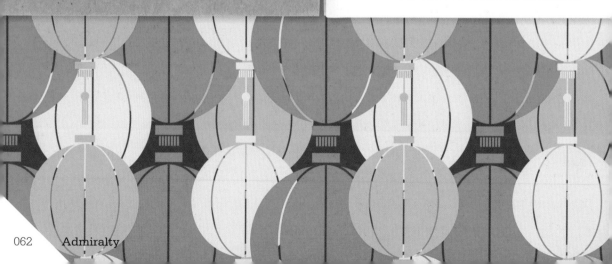

I always make sure I speak to the locals to find interesting spots.

What are your favourite Hong Kong eating and drinking venues?

Ronin (*see* p. 143) has arguably the best Japanese omakase (where the chef decides what you eat) in town in the least pretentious setting, and Soho's Vbest Tea House (*see* map on p. 037) has great home-style Cantonese. For drinks, I love Salon Number 10, in Central, for its quirky interior and intimate live performances, or the newish Ping Pong 129 in Sai Ying Pun.

Where do you escape to when the city gets too much?

I hike around the Tai Tam Reservoir, relax at Big Wave Beach in Shek O on Hong Kong Island, or indulge in a spa treatment at the Grand Hyatt's Plateau Spa in Wan Chai.

Once a sleepy Chinese coastal fishing village, Wan Chai, on Hong Kong Island's northern shore, is now one of the busiest commercial hubs in Hong Kong. Its transformation, thanks mostly to huge land reclamation, also makes it one of the most intriguing haunts for visitors. Revel in the cross-section of dilapidated old shophouses, market streets, residential high-rises, fancy big-brand hotels and behemoth government buildings.

More recently, the restaurant, bar and boutique scene, most of it around Star Street, St Francis Yard and Ship Street, has given Wan Chai another, more contemporary angle.

Wan Chai Station; Admiralty Station

TO WOOLOOMOOLOO
(NOT SHOWN ON MAP)

Ruttonjee Hospital Garden

The Zenith

Wanchai Market

MCGREGOR STREET

TAI YUEN STREET

WAN CHAI ROAD

QUEEN'S ROAD EAST

STONE NULLAH TAVERN

SHEK KAI LANE

KING SING STREET

BLUE HOUSE

YEN WAH STEPS

WAN CHAI VISUAL ARCHIVE

HING WAN STREET

STREET

TAI LUNG FUNG

WAN CHAI GAP ROAD

STONE NULLAH STREET

KAT ON STREET

LUNG ON STREET

KENNEDY STREET

KENNEDY ROAD

KENNEDY ROAD

24   JUN 8076

SHOP

1 Kapok
2 Architectz' Factory
3 Monocle
4 nLostnFound
5 Sau Wa Fong
6 WDSG

WAN CHAI

EAT

7 Rabbithole

EAT AND DRINK

8 Fook Lam Moon
9 22 Ships
10 Bo Innovation
11 Wooloomooloo

LOCKHART ROAD

Lockhart Road Playground

Asia Orient Tower

STREET

LOCKHART

7-Eleven

ROAD

ARSENAL STREET

HENNESSY

N

Empire Hotel Hong Kong

FENWICK

ROAD

MTR Island Line

TO WOOLOOMOOLOO
(NOT SHOWN ON MAP)

JOHNSTON

STREET

STREET

HENNESSY

ROAD

7-Eleven

ROAD

Hong Kong Tramways

FENWICK STREET

7-Eleven

THOMSON

ROAD

QUEEN'S

ANTON

STREET

LANDALE

STREET

RABBITHOLE

灣仔
WAN CHAI

Post office

FOOK LAM MOON

LUARD

WING LOK LANE

ROAD

LI CHIT

STREET

PETIT BAZAAR

GRESSON

STREET

KAPOK

SUN STREET

EAST

FAT

STREET

HAM & SHERRY

BO INNOVATION

THE PAWN

NLOSTNFOUND

KAPOK

ST. FRANCIS YARD

WDSG

SAU WA FONG

LUN

STREET

7-Eleven

SHIP

STREET

MOON STREET

MONOCLE

ODD ONE OUT

TAI WONG STREET WEST

TED'S LOOKOUT

STAR

ST. FRANCIS

SAU WA FONG

ARCHITECTZ' FACTORY

22 SHIPS

TAI WONG STREET EAST

STAR STREET

STREET

JOUER ATELIER'S

SCHOONER STREET

SIK ON STREET

QUEEN'S

ROAD

HILL SIDE TERRACE

HUNG SHING TEMPLE

EAST

(CONT)
TAVERN

JUN 8076

NAM KOU TERRACE

HAU FUNG LANE

TO STONE NULLAH TAVERN & TAI LUNG FUNG
(SEE MAP LEFT)

ROAD

Hopewell Centre

KENNEDY

ROAD

0   100 m

BOWEN

ROAD

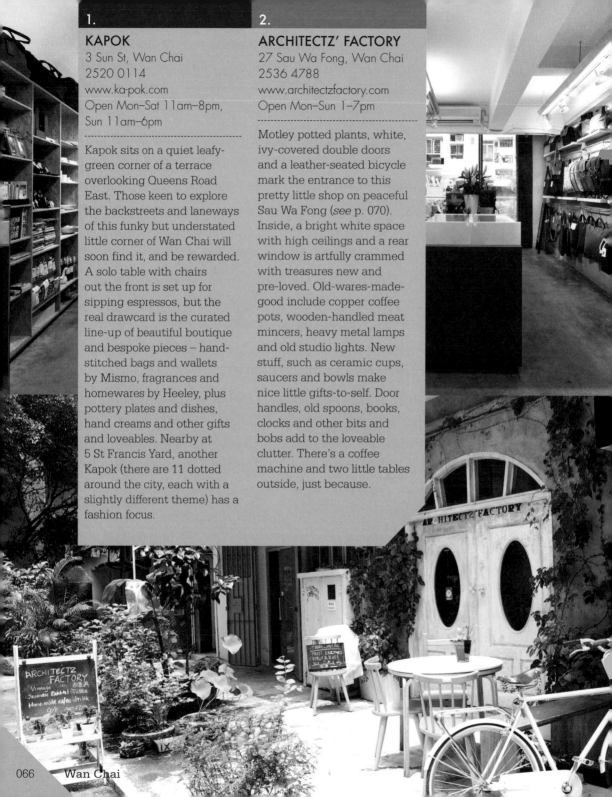

1.

KAPOK

3 Sun St, Wan Chai
2520 0114
www.ka-pok.com
Open Mon–Sat 11am–8pm,
Sun 11am–6pm

Kapok sits on a quiet leafy-green corner of a terrace overlooking Queens Road East. Those keen to explore the backstreets and laneways of this funky but understated little corner of Wan Chai will soon find it, and be rewarded. A solo table with chairs out the front is set up for sipping espressos, but the real drawcard is the curated line-up of beautiful boutique and bespoke pieces – hand-stitched bags and wallets by Mismo, fragrances and homewares by Heeley, plus pottery plates and dishes, hand creams and other gifts and loveables. Nearby at 5 St Francis Yard, another Kapok (there are 11 dotted around the city, each with a slightly different theme) has a fashion focus.

2.

ARCHITECTZ' FACTORY

27 Sau Wa Fong, Wan Chai
2536 4788
www.architectzfactory.com
Open Mon–Sun 1–7pm

Motley potted plants, white, ivy-covered double doors and a leather-seated bicycle mark the entrance to this pretty little shop on peaceful Sau Wa Fong (*see* p. 070). Inside, a bright white space with high ceilings and a rear window is artfully crammed with treasures new and pre-loved. Old-wares-made-good include copper coffee pots, wooden-handled meat mincers, heavy metal lamps and old studio lights. New stuff, such as ceramic cups, saucers and bowls make nice little gifts-to-self. Door handles, old spoons, books, clocks and other bits and bobs add to the loveable clutter. There's a coffee machine and two little tables outside, just because.

1.

2.

1.

1.

2.

2.

3.

MONOCLE

1–4 St Francis Yard, Wan Chai
2804 2323
www.monocle.com
Open Mon–Sat 11am–7pm,
Sun 12–6pm

Unapologetically highbrow, aesthetically snobbish and eternally elitist, Monocle lives and breathes the company theme – quality of life – with impeccable style. The brand's Hong Kong 'bureau' is part sleek office, part teeny boutique. Subscribe to the eponymous magazine or shop for your metrosexual man. Gifts include grey-ceramic and bamboo, eco-friendly teapot sets by Cuckoo (with a lid that doubles as a cup), and signature Gemma wooden boxes with magnetic lids by Discipline, perfect for keeping cufflinks in. Less functional but typically intriguing is the lovely hardcover *Art Lover's Guide to Japanese Museums*.

NLOSTNFOUND

3 St Francis Yard, Wan Chai
2574 1328
www.nlostnfound.com
Open Mon–Sat 1–8pm,
Sun 1–6pm

- -

The long-closed attic of a
stately old colonial home has
been emptied into this shop
– or so you'd think. In a city
that loves brand spanking
new, this treasure trove of
curios and memorabilia is
a one-of-a-kind find. Old
children's leather satchels,
cane prams and metal wind-
up toys sit beside 1970s retro
kitchen clocks, Art Deco side
tables and old Air France
suitcases. Flick through
piles of *Tintin* comics and
collectible records, or dust off
the covers of leather-bound
books with front pages that
sport the names of previous
owners in big cursive
writing. It's like the shopping
equivalent of slow food.

5.

SAU WA FONG
Wan Chai

As St Francis Yard and Star Street inevitably start to attract bigger brands, keep your eye on Sau Wa Fong as the next boutique street. Its gorgeous, well-lit gaggle of shops beneath low-rise buildings are an anomaly, with no traffic save for ambling pedestrians and the odd cat. The shops tend to have an endearing curiosity about them. Interior-design store **Lala Curio** sells insect plates, brass animal heads and harlequin sideboards. **Jouer Atelier's** mini macarons come in local flavours including Hong Kong milk tea and Chinese vinegar and ginger. **Odd One Out** is an exhibition space selling a collection of artful ceramics – and coffee. Architectz' Factory (_see_ p. 066) is here too.

WDSG

9 St Francis St, Wan Chai
2528 3800
www.wd-sg.com
Open Mon–Sun 12–9pm

From the sloping footpath, WDSG, a mostly men's clothing store founded by Ken Suen (*see* p. 212) looks tiny. But inside, stairs lead down to a large cavernous space as quiet as a library and with the ambience of a museum. The tendency is to tiptoe. Overcome this and there's plenty to take in. The focus feels American rootsie, with bandanas, highly polished leather boots, shirts, jeans and overalls. The tailoring and heavy fabrics – thick cotton and denim – translate into contemporary workwear. As is the trend, the decor here blends seamlessly with the fashion and you'll find yourself lifting the ceramic teacups and old wares to see if you can take them home.

RABBITHOLE
3 Landale St, Wan Chai
2528 0039
www.rabbitholecoffee.com
Open Mon–Fri 8am–8pm,
Sat–Sun 9am–8pm

Dim lighting, industrial tables and understated decor only serve to heighten the most important piece of apparatus in this hidey-hole cafe – the coffee machine. While the local antipodean population is largely responsible for bringing lattes to Hong Kong, Rabbithole has taken the bean fetish one caffeinated step further. It serves Japanese-style hand-drip coffee from mad-scientist-looking flasks, and bags of hand-selected beans for punters to take home. Two blends are available each day, including the slightly more expensive daily grind, and there's also a small selection of pastries and sandwiches. Tip for neophytes: don't go asking for decaf.

8.

FOOK LAM MOON

43–45 Johnston Rd, Wan Chai
2866 0663
www.fooklammoon-grp.com
Open Mon–Sun 11.30am–
3pm & 6–11pm

Whelk (a saltwater mollusc), shark's fin, bird's nest, abalone: if it's traditional Cantonese gastronomy you're after, the Chui family restaurant, opened in 1972, is where it's still at to this day. This four-storey place with the requisite round tables, chandeliers, carved wood panels and serious staff is the self-professed restaurant for the city's elite. Tycoons, politicians and celebrities front up here to spend big money on the luxurious ingredients, of which millions of dollars worth are said to be in stock at any one time. For the rest of us, equally traditional dishes include roast suckling pig and crispy chicken.

9.

22 SHIPS

22 Ship St, Wan Chai
2555 0722
www.22ships.hk
Open Mon–Sat 12–3pm &
6–11pm, Sun 12–2.30pm &
6–10pm

Before 22 Ships opened its ubercool doors, Ship Street was a foodie haunt for only those in the know. But the area has transformed in no time. This 'bar de tapa', with a central kitchen and bar stools positioned so customers can oversee the food prepping, is one of a dozen or so places primed for delivering food of an international standard. UK chef Jason Atherton serves creative takes on Spanish ingredients: ibérico pork and foie-gras hamburgers; jamon, manchego cheese and truffle toasties; goat's cheese ice-cream for dessert. In true southern Spanish style, this place has a list of sherries, including a drop or two sourced from the famed El Bulli cellar in Spain.

8.

9.

HOT TIP
Down the road from 22 Ships is sister Spanish bar Ham & Sherry (1–7 Ship Street). It has similarly fabulous tapas and does sherry pairings. 'Pica Pica' snack hour from 5pm to 6pm is a cheap way to taste a variety of small dishes. ¡Que aproveche! (Enjoy!)

BO INNOVATION

Shop 13, Level 2, J Residence,
60 Johnston Rd (lift entrance
18 Ship St), Wan Chai
2850 8371
www.boinnovation.com
Open Mon–Fri 12–3pm &
7pm–12am, Sat 6pm–12am

Don't let the slightly cheesy catchline 'X-treme Chinese Cuisine' turn you off. This is Hong Kong's answer to the UK's Fat Duck. Instead of Heston Blumenthal, you'll find someone equally big on personality, Alvin Leung (*see* p. 082), who gives new life to traditional Chinese food and incorporates non-Chinese ingredients into centuries-old recipes. His rock'n'roll appearance (tats, purple hair) gives the place extra dynamism, but the food speaks for itself. Takes on Cantonese favourites include molecular xiao long bao (soup dumplings) and taro nest made from smoked quail eggs topped with caviar. A seat at the chef's table is worth the money, and if you get this far, you should lash out and opt for wine pairing – another thrill for the palate.

WOOLOOMOOLOO
Rooftop, The Hennessy,
256 Hennessy Rd, Wan Chai
2893 6960
www.wooloo-mooloo.com
Open Mon–Sun 11.45am–
2.30pm & 6pm–late

When 'no smoking' regulations hit Hong Kong a few years back, outdoor entertaining suddenly became vogue for the otherwise air-conditioner-loving population. The upshot for the city's social set, be they smokers or not, was a rush of open-air bars and alfresco eateries. The best are found on rooftops teetering above the bright lights below. Wooloomooloo bar, a one-stop elevator ride from the notable steak and grill restaurant below, is a vertigo-inducing example. Wooden decking, an oversized cuddle-up couch and a cocktail list as long as my arm are second only to the rock-star views stretching from Victoria Harbour to Happy Valley racecourse. Add some dance tunes and this is the place to be from 6pm.

12.
STONE NULLAH TAVERN
69 Stone Nullah La, Wan Chai
3182 0128
www.stonenullahtavern.com
Open Tues–Sun 6–11pm

In a characteristic little pocket of Wan Chai still inhabited by mechanics' garages and mom-and-pop shops, Stone Nullah Tavern has become somewhat of a 'local'. The front bar has high tables and an indoor–outdoor vibe perfect for after-work drinks. The rear dining room is part American barn, part farmhouse, with pressed metal ceilings, vintage lighting, a leather bench seat and bookshelves. The cuisine is 'new American'. Pair a mac-and-cheese (mixed with an egg yolk at your table) with American craft tap beers, or go for crispy pig's head (brine-soaked for six days, braised for six hours, turned into a terrine, then breaded and fried) with lubricating boutique bourbon.

13.
TAI LUNG FUNG
5 Hing Wan St, Wan Chai
2572 0055
Open Mon–Sat 12pm–12am

Welcome to Hong Kong, circa 1960. This cute, low-key bar, at the bottom of an old tong lau (tenement) building, playfully pays homage to a bygone era. The retro fit-out – best viewed at night – starts with Chinese lanterns and a pink neon-lit street sign. Indoors, it's similarly moody, low-lit with plastic light shades and adorned with retro curiosities – old paper clippings, oversized papier-mâché Chinese opera masks, clocks stuck in time and vintage public-service posters. The small tiled bar has stools for indulging in TLF signature cocktails made with home-brewed Puer whisky, and osmanthus (a native woodland shrub) and lemongrass liqueurs. There are four or five beers on tap.

12.

13.

HOT TIP
Above Tai Lung Fung is the Wan Chai Visual Archive. Around the corner is the gorgeous Blue House heritage building. Both are worthy of a drop-in.

14.

TED'S LOOKOUT

Moonful Crt, 17A Moon St,
Wan Chai
2520 0076
www.facebook.com/pages/
teds-lookout/
344402725647941
Open Mon–Sun 12–11pm

There is no Ted, nor is there a lookout. In fact, the enclosed nature of this tucked-away urban bar is part of its intimate appeal. The look is industrial chic, with rusted-metal window frames and concrete walls softened by retro cinema seats, bentwood stools, white bar tiles and miners' lanterns set to dim. American-style burgers are the go for lunch. Latino comes later in the day – try a taco platter with chorizo, beef, fish and tiger-prawn flavours, plus sides of spicy barbecued corn and buffalo wings. With a limited wine list, this is the place for Cuban cocktails, such as the Pisco Sour Reborn or Blood de Caribbean.

15.

THE PAWN

62 Johnston Rd, Wan Chai
2866 3444
www.thepawn.com.hk
Open Mon–Sun 12–11pm

Few places in Hong Kong retain the character of colonial times. Here, G&Ts are sipped in cane chairs while trams rattle past like they have done for a century. This old-style, four-abreast shophouse conversion is true to past and present. It has a chair-crammed balcony and bar on one level (serving fish and chips, Welsh rarebit, devils on horseback, half pint of prawns) with a whisky list of the finest Scottish drops. There's a vintage cigar selection, and see the champagne list for a bottle of Pol Roger Winston Churchill Épernay 2000, by Jove! Upstairs the formal dining room has a British fine-dining menu. As this book went to print, the Pawn was undergoing a makeover. Expect something equally good.

14.

15.

Alvin Leung might have been born in England and raised in Canada, but he calls Hong Kong home. His restaurant, Bo Innovation (see p. 076), is famed for taking traditional Chinese flavours and ingredients and updating them with contemporary techniques and pairings. Last year Bo was one of only five Hong Kong restaurants to be awarded the coveted three Michelin stars.

How do you define Hong Kong's dining scene?

It is one of the best in the world. Not only does it have the best of the East, in terms of variety and authenticity, but it also has really great French, Italian, Middle Eastern, Spanish and every other culture's cuisine. You can't say that about many countries. You probably can't find very good roasted duck or a chiu chow crab (from Guangdong province) in France or Italy, for example.

Where do you like to drink in Hong Kong?

I'm too old to party in Lan Kwai Fong (see p. 024) so I usually stick to nice quiet bars in hotels, preferably with an outdoor terrace so I can smoke one of my five-a-day cigars. Namely, places like the Waterfall Bar and poolside Grill at Wan Chai's Grand Hyatt.

Where do you go for good Cantonese food?

For really cheap, good and fast food, I like Sheung Kee at Wong Nai Chung Market (*see* p. 094). For a more luxurious dinner when someone else is paying, I'd choose Celebrity Cuisine at the Lan Kwai Fong Hotel in Sheung Wan (*see* map on p. 127).

Map labels

Causeway Bay Sports Ground

Hong Kong Central Library

CLASSIFIED

LAB MADE ICE CREAM

UNAR COFFEE

FEEL SO GOOD

PAPABUBBLE

大坑

TAI HANG

FIRE DRAGON PATH

TUNG LO WAN ROAD

TUNG LO WAN ROAD

WUN SHA STREET

SCHOOL STREET

KING STREET

WARREN STREET

ORMSBY STREET

SUN CHUN STREET

TAI HANG ROAD

KA NING PATH

TAI HANG ROAD

Known as Pow Ma Dai or 'horserace place', Happy Valley is famed for its inner-city racecourse and associated high-spirited festivities (*see* p. 092). The unique green space, looped by a tram track, hams up the village atmosphere of this popular residential hub on Hong Kong Island. The main thoroughfare, Sing Woo Road, boasts Cantonese gems such as Wong Nai Chung Market (*see* p. 094) and Dim Sum (*see* p. 090).

A 20-minute walk away, over Morrison Hill, Tai Hang is a different scene again. Once the stronghold of garages and car repairers, this clutch of characteristic low-rise buildings has been reborn as a nocturnal hangout (don't bother coming before 3pm).

Tin Hau Station
(Tai Hang only)

24   JUN 8OT6

SHOP
1   THE GURUS SHOP
2   PAPABUBBLE
EAT
3   UNAR COFFEE
4   LAB MADE ICE CREAM

17

EAT AND DRINK
5   CLASSIFIED
6   DIM SUM
7   HAPPY VALLEY RACES
8   HMV KAFÉ
9   WONG NAI CHUNG MARKET
10 SAINT-GERMAIN

HAPPY VALLEY AND TAI HANG

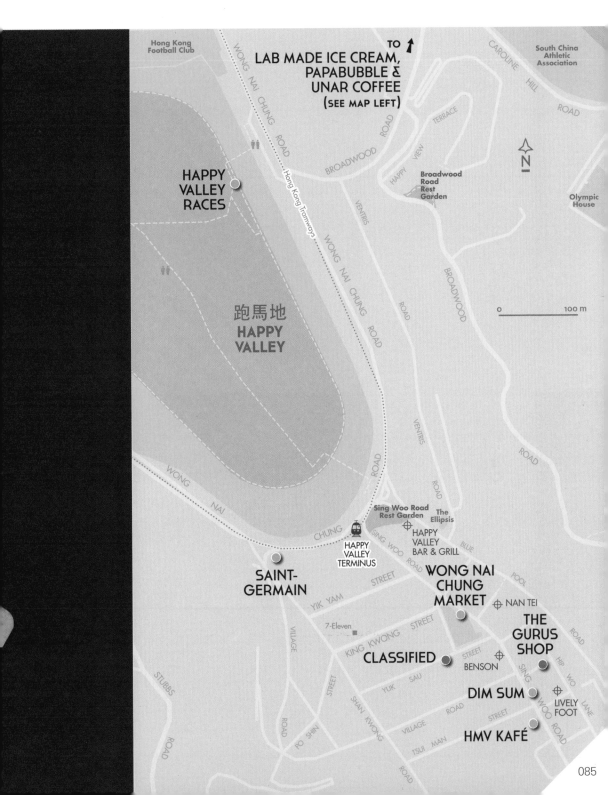

Hong Kong Football Club

TO ↑
LAB MADE ICE CREAM,
PAPABUBBLE &
UNAR COFFEE
(SEE MAP LEFT)

CAROLINE HILL ROAD

South China Athletic Association

WONG NAI CHUNG ROAD

BROADWOOD ROAD

TERRACE

HAPPY VIEW TERRACE

Broadwood Road Rest Garden

N

Olympic House

HAPPY VALLEY RACES

VENTRIS ROAD

WONG NAI CHUNG ROAD

BROADWOOD ROAD

Hong Kong Tramways

跑馬地
HAPPY VALLEY

0   100 m

WONG NAI

CHUNG

VENTRIS ROAD

ROAD

ROAD

ROAD

Sing Woo Road Rest Garden

The Ellipsis

HAPPY VALLEY BAR & GRILL

BLUE POOL ROAD

HAPPY VALLEY TERMINUS

SING WOO ROAD

SAINT-GERMAIN

WONG NAI CHUNG MARKET

NAN TEI

STREET

YIK YAM STREET

VILLAGE

7-Eleven

KING KWONG STREET

STREET

THE GURUS SHOP

CLASSIFIED

BENSON

SING WOO ROAD

HIP WO LANE

DIM SUM

LIVELY FOOT

STUBBS ROAD

ROAD

PO SHIN STREET

SHAN KWONG ROAD

YUK SAU STREET

VILLAGE

TSUI MAN STREET

WONG NAI CHUNG ROAD

HMV KAFÉ

1.

THE GURUS SHOP
8 Cheong Ming St,
Happy Valley
2891 0138
www.gurus.hk
Open Mon–Sun 11am–8pm

Big Boys' Toys could be another name for the Gurus Shop. This contemporary place with window-shopper-friendly floor-to-ceiling glass is a nifty-gifty shop for the (very) well-off man about town. Leica cameras, coloured binoculars, Rolex watches and Dyson propeller-less fans are stylish and practical, but you can let loose with some downright hedonistic things: the Angry Lego motorbike helmet holders, for example. More eccentric items for those with more money than sense include the Darcel, Colette & Vipp toilet cleaner and Renova sexiest toilet paper. The bee's knees of gifts is surely the Romain Jerome moon DNA watches, which are made with parts of the *Apollo 11* spacecraft. They'll set you back about one million Hongky dollars.

2.

PAPABUBBLE
Shop 1, 34 Tung Lo Wan Rd,
Tai Hang
2367 4807
www.papabubble.com.hk
Open Mon–Sun 11am–10pm

They call themselves 'caramel artisans' but 'boiled sweets artisans' is probably more like it. Either way, this Spanish franchise bordering Tai Hang and Causeway Bay is the only one of its kind in Hong Kong and is the love child of friendly owner Ammy Ho. Through perspex screens you can watch staff roll great wads of colourful caramel goo into the shape of the sweets, or pop in and out for a little bag of suckable souvenirs. There are myriad flavours and designs. Some come with 'I love HK' written on them, others with the iconic double happiness Chinese character. The sweetest tooth might opt for an oversized lollypop.

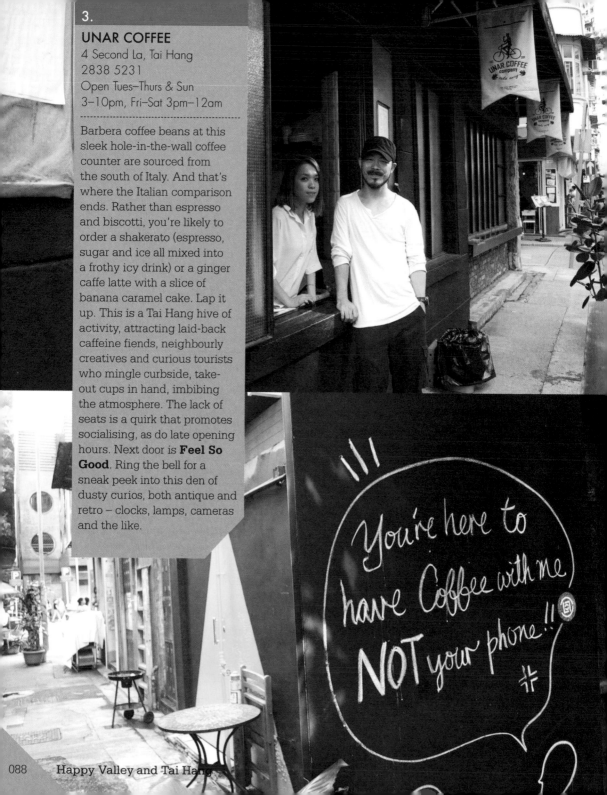

3.

UNAR COFFEE

4 Second La, Tai Hang
2838 5231
Open Tues–Thurs & Sun
3–10pm, Fri–Sat 3pm–12am

Barbera coffee beans at this
sleek hole-in-the-wall coffee
counter are sourced from
the south of Italy. And that's
where the Italian comparison
ends. Rather than espresso
and biscotti, you're likely to
order a shakerato (espresso,
sugar and ice all mixed into
a frothy icy drink) or a ginger
caffe latte with a slice of
banana caramel cake. Lap it
up. This is a Tai Hang hive of
activity, attracting laid-back
caffeine fiends, neighbourly
creatives and curious tourists
who mingle curbside, take-
out cups in hand, imbibing
the atmosphere. The lack of
seats is a quirk that promotes
socialising, as do late opening
hours. Next door is **Feel So
Good**. Ring the bell for a
sneak peek into this den of
dusty curios, both antique and
retro – clocks, lamps, cameras
and the like.

LAB MADE ICE CREAM

6 Brown St, Tai Hang
www.labmade.com.hk
Open Tues–Thurs 3pm–12am,
Fri 3pm–1am, Sat 1pm–1am,
Sun 1–11pm

It takes a special kind of nerd to turn ice-cream making into a scientific endeavour, but we are ever so grateful to the folks behind Lab Made. This ice-cream purveyor uses extremely cold liquid nitrogen (-196°C if you must know) to rapidly freeze its ingredients, which results in smaller ice crystals than commercial varieties and smooth, creamy ice-cream. The novelty is, it only takes 60 seconds to freeze, so customers can hang around and watch the process. And they do. The darkened faux-laboratory shop fit-out, industrial-sized mixers, lab-coated staff and clouds of billowing liquid nitrogen all make for the kind of fun that appeals to students and pimply teens. The weekly revolving flavours will appeal to everyone: get local with Hong Kong pineapple bun, lychee yoghurt and longan, or Horlicks malt with wheat cream.

5.

CLASSIFIED

Kam Yuk Mansion,
13 Yuk Sau St, Happy Valley
2891 3454
www.classifiedfoodshops.com.hk
Open Mon–Sun 8am–12am

When Classified the Cheese Room first opened in Sheung Wan, it was one of few reliable European cafes in Hong Kong. Similar manifestations with less emphasis on cheese soon opened. Today continental cafe culture is easier to find, but Classified still holds its own for reliably good breakfasts (poached eggs royale with smoked salmon and hollandaise sauce) and all-day dining (toasted ciabatta, steak frites, tiger-prawn linguine). Cheese and charcuterie platters are also popular. The Happy Valley cafe is open-fronted with share tables and a rear terrace. There's also a branch in **Tai Hang** (1–9 Lin Fa Kung Street West; *see* map on p. 084); it's on a corner, great for people-watching. Both are industrial chic in design.

6.

DIM SUM

63 Sing Woo Rd, Happy Valley
2834 8893
Open Mon–Fri 11am–11pm,
Sat–Sun 10.30am–11pm

It's Yu Man Fang to the locals, but if you can't read Cantonese you'll probably recognise it as Dim Sum (these words glow on a green neon sign out the front). Sitting on a nondescript strip towards the top end of Sing Woo Road, this homely family run restaurant has a colonial interior with high ceilings, fans, wood-carved booths and a menu full of pictures for easy ordering. It's well known for serving 'the art of Chinese titbits', such as dim sum that includes quality har gow (shrimp dumplings) and gin cheun fan (pan-fried rice rolls), available day and night. The à la carte menu has Western favourites such as beef with black-bean sauce and sweet-and-sour pork. Adding to the nostalgia, Coca-Cola comes in glass bottles. There's Tsingtao beer, but BYO wine.

5.

HOT TIP
Beginning at the roundabout where Blue Pool Road meets Stubbs Road in Happy Valley, Bowen Road path is a popular walkway that weaves through rainforest and past picturesque viewpoints all the way to Admiralty.

6.

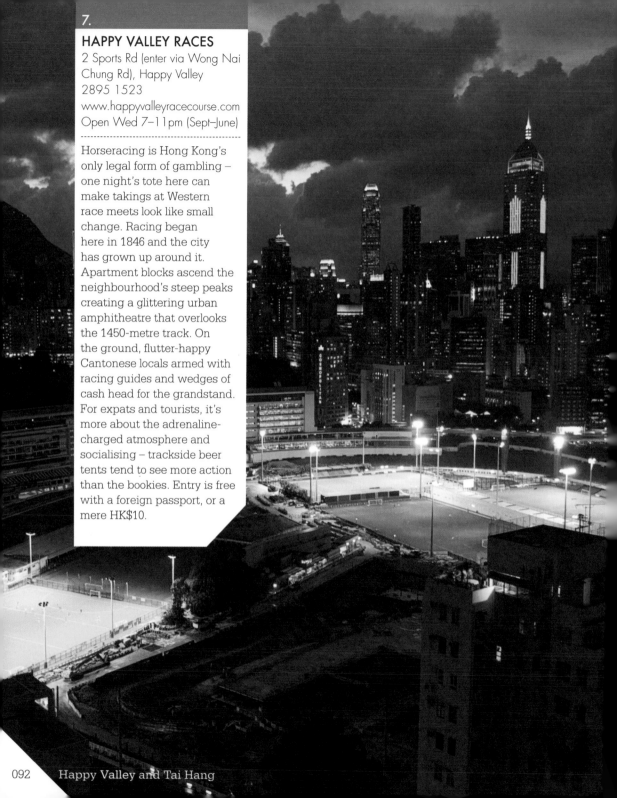

7.

HAPPY VALLEY RACES

2 Sports Rd (enter via Wong Nai
Chung Rd), Happy Valley
2895 1523
www.happyvalleyracecourse.com
Open Wed 7–11pm (Sept–June)

Horseracing is Hong Kong's
only legal form of gambling –
one night's tote here can
make takings at Western
race meets look like small
change. Racing began
here in 1846 and the city
has grown up around it.
Apartment blocks ascend the
neighbourhood's steep peaks
creating a glittering urban
amphitheatre that overlooks
the 1450-metre track. On
the ground, flutter-happy
Cantonese locals armed with
racing guides and wedges of
cash head for the grandstand.
For expats and tourists, it's
more about the adrenaline-
charged atmosphere and
socialising – trackside beer
tents tend to see more action
than the bookies. Entry is free
with a foreign passport, or a
mere HK$10.

HMV KAFÉ
18A Sing Woo Rd,
Happy Valley
2891 8558
www.hmvkafe.com
Open Mon–Thurs 10am–12am,
Fri 10am–2am, Sat 9.30am–
2am, Sun 9.30am–12am

It's early days for concept stores in Hong Kong and HMV Kafé is still adjusting. Is it a music store? A bar? A cafe? A restaurant? It doesn't really matter. The heavy artillery Simonelli coffee machine here produces the best cafe latte in Happy Valley, and the causally cool decor is an eye on how the local latte set likes it. Bottles of red wine and rows of top 10 CDs line the counter. Elsewhere, books, magazines and Nirvana, Coldplay and Blur CDs identify the owners as Gen X. Beatles pictures and music-inspired coffee drinks such as a Ray Charles 'blues' iced coffee with espresso, cola and lime juice continue the harmonious theme. Eats include thin-based pizzas, burgers and eggs Benny.

9.

WONG NAI CHUNG MARKET

Level 3, cnr Yuk Sau St and
Sing Woo Rd, Happy Valley
2822 2994
Open Mon–Sun 6pm–12am

There's nothing overly eye-catching about this large shared eating area, located on the top floor of a municipal council building and accessed via a lift on Sing Woo Road. But who cares about plastic-fantastic fixed chairs and toilet-role serviettes when you're about to eat your weight in good nosh? This is 100% Cantonese cuisine, the way local families love it. When you step out of the lift, head to **Sheung Kee**; it's on the right and is the better of the two eateries here. Choose from huge prawns and fresh fish flapping around in plastic tubs or go straight to the abridged English menu for pork neck, garlic-encrusted roast chicken or eggplant (aubergine) and minced-pork hotpot. The local Tsingtao beer is served in a longneck bottle.

SAINT-GERMAIN

1A Wong Nai Chung Rd,
Happy Valley
2836 6131
www.french-creations.com/
saint-germain
Open Mon–Sun 12pm–12am

Hong Kong's French population of 16,000 is the largest in Asia, so it's no surprise that French cuisine in Hong Kong can be as good as that from France. Saint-Germain is no exception. This hidey-hole Parisian-style brasserie, which bookends one end of the famed Happy Valley racecourse, has a following of local expats who sit on bentwood stools at high tables drinking and listening to jazz. Alternatively there are booths down the back surrounded by mirrored walls and a chequered floor. The fare is so French it's almost clichéd. Specials are chalked up on a blackboard, such as homemade duck rillettes served with gherkins, snails in garlic and parsley butter, and entrecote de boeuf with frites and pepper sauce. The posh beer glasses win me over every time. Every. Single. Time.

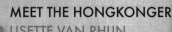

MEET THE HONGKONGER
LISETTE VAN RHIJN
URBAN DISCOVERY
APP WRITER

Originally from the Netherlands, Lisette van Rhijn moved to Hong Kong six years ago and quickly found that behind the glass-and-concrete facade were inspiring, vibrant and authentic neighbourhoods. She began working with Urban Discovery, a social enterprise that creates awareness of built heritage in Asian cities through initiatives such as the iDiscover city walk app (http://i-discoverasia.com). Lisette lives in Happy Valley.

What is your favourite Hong Kong neighbourhood?

Our first app destination: Sham Shui Po, on the Kowloon peninsula. It is one of the city's oldest and poorest neighbourhoods, with typical Hong Kong entrepreneurship, surprising art communities and lots of local colour and flavour.

What are your favourite places in Happy Valley?

On Wednesday nights during racing season we can literally cheer on the horses from our balcony! I also love good, cheap foot massages at Lively Foot, and eating yakitori (grilled skewered chicken) at Nan Tei or French at Benson. Happy Valley Bar & Grill is another local love-in (*see* map on p. 085 for all four of these venues).

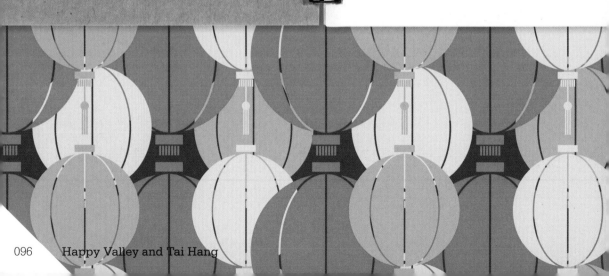

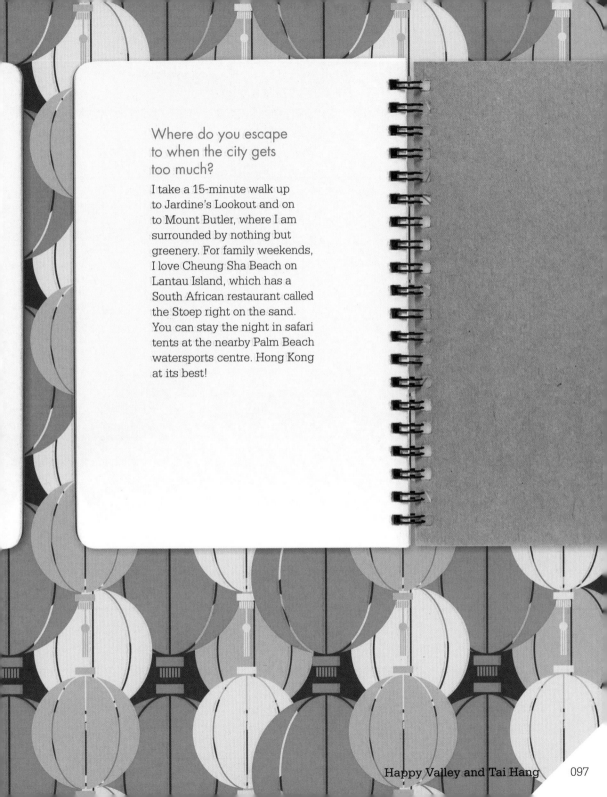

Where do you escape to when the city gets too much?

I take a 15-minute walk up to Jardine's Lookout and on to Mount Butler, where I am surrounded by nothing but greenery. For family weekends, I love Cheung Sha Beach on Lantau Island, which has a South African restaurant called the Stoep right on the sand. You can stay the night in safari tents at the nearby Palm Beach watersports centre. Hong Kong at its best!

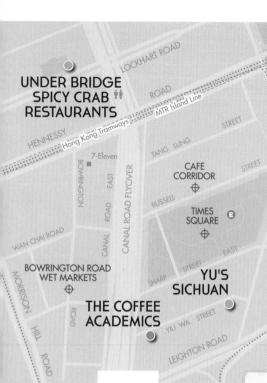

UNDER BRIDGE SPICY CRAB RESTAURANTS

LOCKHART ROAD

HENNESSY

Hong Kong Tramways

MTR Island Line

ROAD

STREET

7-Eleven

BOWRINGTON

CANAL ROAD FLYOVER

TANG LUNG

CAFE CORRIDOR

STREET

EAST

RUSSELL

ROAD

CANAL

WAN CHAI ROAD

TIMES SQUARE

EAST

BOWRINGTON ROAD WET MARKETS

SHARP

STREET

YU'S SICHUAN

MORRISON

THE COFFEE ACADEMICS

HILL

ROAD

YIU WA STREET

LEIGHTON ROAD

CAUSEWAY BAY

Money doesn't burn a hole in your pocket for long in Causeway Bay. This excessively built-up Hong Kong Island suburb is a shopper's paradise, a neon-lit, pedestrian-clad hub with every inch dedicated if not to materialism then certainly commercialism.

It caters to all budgets and desires with luxury mega malls, such as Hysan Place (*see* p. 100) and Times Square, mid-range department stores (Sogo), street markets, wet markets and hundreds of one-off shops selling clothes, shoes, electronics, computers, skincare products, you name it. At the eastern end, Victoria Park is its green lung – worth strolling through once you've maxed-out your MasterCard.

Causeway Bay Station

24   JUN 8DT6

SHOP

1   HOMELESS
2   HYSAN PLACE
3   I.T.
4   LOVERAMICS
5   LUDDITE
6   PATERSON, KINGSTON & CLEVELAND STREETS

17

EAT

7   18 GRAMS
8   THE COFFEE ACADEMICS

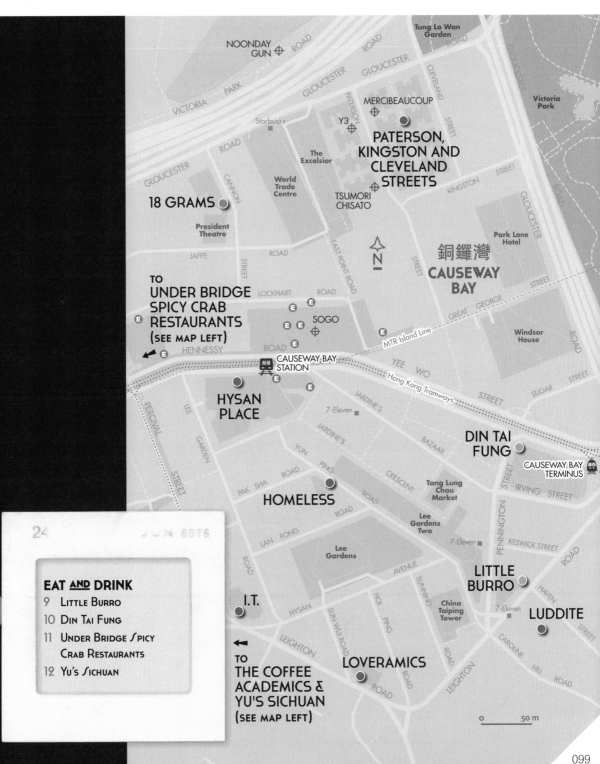

NOONDAY GUN ⊕ ROAD

Tung Lo Wan Garden

GLOUCESTER ROAD

VICTORIA PARK

GLOUCESTER ROAD

CLEVELAND STREET

GLOUCESTER ROAD

Victoria Park

Starbucks ■

PATERSON STREET

MERCIBEAUCOUP

Y3 ⊕

PATERSON, KINGSTON AND CLEVELAND STREETS

The Excelsior

World Trade Centre

TSUMORI CHISATO ⊕

KINGSTON STREET

Park Lane Hotel

GLOUCESTER ROAD

18 GRAMS ●

CANNON STREET

President Theatre

JAFFE ROAD

STREET

ROAD

EAST POINT ROAD

↑N

STREET

銅鑼灣 **CAUSEWAY BAY**

Windsor House

TO UNDER BRIDGE SPICY CRAB RESTAURANTS (SEE MAP LEFT)

LOCKHART ROAD

Ⓔ Ⓔ

Ⓔ Ⓔ SOGO ⊕

Ⓔ

GREAT GEORGE STREET

ROAD

← Ⓔ HENNESSY ROAD

Ⓔ

MTR Island Line

YEE WO STREET

SUGAR STREET

CAUSEWAY BAY STATION 🚇

Ⓔ

Hong Kong Tramways

HYSAN PLACE

PERCIVAL STREET

LEE GARDEN

Ⓔ

JARDINE'S

7-Eleven ■

JARDINE'S

BAZAAR

DIN TAI FUNG

STREET

IRVING STREET

CAUSEWAY BAY TERMINUS 🚋

YUN PING ROAD

PAK SHA ROAD

HOMELESS ●

CRESCENT

Tang Lung Chau Market

Lee Gardens Two

7-Eleven ■

PENNINGTON STREET

KESWICK STREET

LAN FONG ROAD

Lee Gardens

AVENUE

SUNNING ROAD

LITTLE BURRO ●

HAVEN STREET

I.T. ●

HYSAN AVENUE

SUN WUI ROAD

HOI PING ROAD

China Taiping Tower

7-Eleven ■

LUDDITE ●

CAROLINE HILL ROAD

LEIGHTON ROAD

← **TO THE COFFEE ACADEMICS & YU'S SICHUAN** (SEE MAP LEFT)

LOVERAMICS ●

ROAD

LEIGHTON ROAD

24 JUN 8016

EAT AND DRINK
9 LITTLE BURRO
10 DIN TAI FUNG
11 UNDER BRIDGE SPICY CRAB RESTAURANTS
12 YU'S SICHUAN

0   50 m

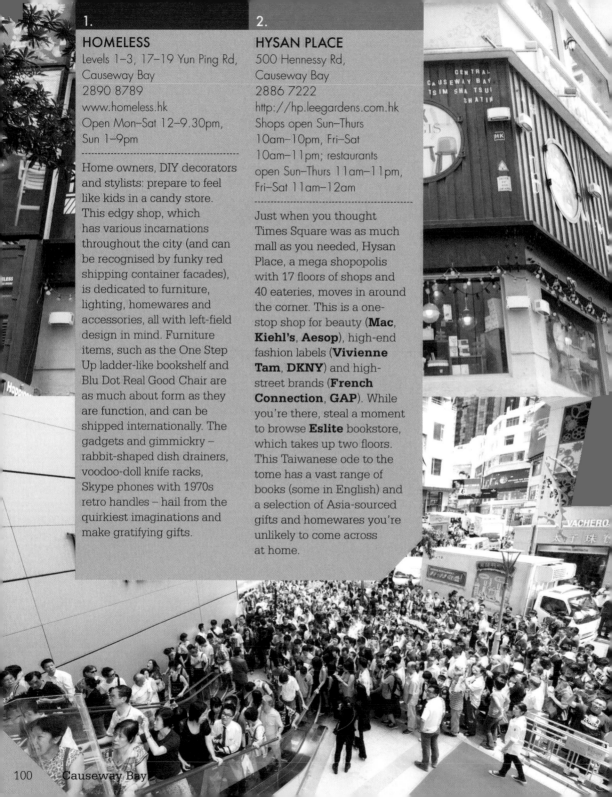

1.

HOMELESS

Levels 1–3, 17–19 Yun Ping Rd,
Causeway Bay
2890 8789
www.homeless.hk
Open Mon–Sat 12–9.30pm,
Sun 1–9pm

Home owners, DIY decorators
and stylists: prepare to feel
like kids in a candy store.
This edgy shop, which
has various incarnations
throughout the city (and can
be recognised by funky red
shipping container facades),
is dedicated to furniture,
lighting, homewares and
accessories, all with left-field
design in mind. Furniture
items, such as the One Step
Up ladder-like bookshelf and
Blu Dot Real Good Chair are
as much about form as they
are function, and can be
shipped internationally. The
gadgets and gimmickry –
rabbit-shaped dish drainers,
voodoo-doll knife racks,
Skype phones with 1970s
retro handles – hail from the
quirkiest imaginations and
make gratifying gifts.

2.

HYSAN PLACE

500 Hennessy Rd,
Causeway Bay
2886 7222
http://hp.leegardens.com.hk
Shops open Sun–Thurs
10am–10pm, Fri–Sat
10am–11pm; restaurants
open Sun–Thurs 11am–11pm,
Fri–Sat 11am–12am

Just when you thought
Times Square was as much
mall as you needed, Hysan
Place, a mega shopopolis
with 17 floors of shops and
40 eateries, moves in around
the corner. This is a one-
stop shop for beauty (**Mac**,
Kiehl's, **Aesop**), high-end
fashion labels (**Vivienne
Tam**, **DKNY**) and high-
street brands (**French
Connection**, **GAP**). While
you're there, steal a moment
to browse **Eslite** bookstore,
which takes up two floors.
This Taiwanese ode to the
tome has a vast range of
books (some in English) and
a selection of Asia-sourced
gifts and homewares you're
unlikely to come across
at home.

Bowrington Road wet markets, two blocks west from Times Square, bustle with locals buying fresh fruit and vegetables, and seafood that still flaps. The open-fronted food shops are excellent for a local lunch and a beer as you watch the world go by.

3.

I.T.
1 Hysan Ave, Causeway Bay
2890 7012
www.ithk.com
Open Mon–Sun 12–10pm

Young folk with a distinctive sense of style and an eye for fun fashion are the focus of mega-successful, Hong Kong–wide, concept brand I.T. The Causeway Bay flagship store is a four-storey eye-catcher with awesome window displays and an architectural interior with sleek walls, glass display cases framed by wood-patterned cement panels, and parquet floors. At night, when most Hongkongers shop, it is lit by fancy spotlights and luminous walls. Got your attention? The stores stock a load of cool labels, both expensive and mid-range, including edgy global brands. What it's most respected for is discovering small names and catapulting them to stardom. Examples include Chocolate, Mini Cream, Beams and Journal Standard.

LOVERAMICS

97 Leighton Rd, Causeway Bay
2915 8018
www.loveramics.com
Open Sun–Thurs 11am–9pm,
Fri–Sat 11am–10pm

'I love ceramics' – you just don't hear that enough. This squeakily modern Hong Kong–born boutique is a temple to ceramic tableware your grandma didn't have. The designers are universal, all artfully chosen for their craftsmanship, creativity, East–West aesthetic and practical edge. Cups, saucers, soy-sauce bowls and soup spoons by Flutter are inspired by classic Chinese hua niao (flower bird) paintings. Auspicious double-coin-symbol retro mugs with wooden lids are the love child of Loveramics' design team and G.O.D. (*see* p. 176). Cups by Crackle are a contemporary interpretation of a classic oriental teacup. Rice bowls by A Curious Toile featuring whimsical quintessential English scenery make the perfect cross-cultural gift.

5.

LUDDITE
15A Haven St, Causeway Bay
2870 0422
www.facebook.com/
luddite1811
Open Mon–Sun 12–9pm

It's rather bizarre stepping from grotty Lei Shun Court into the hipster interior of Luddite, a mostly men's boutique created and sourced by a Hong Kong designer with a passion for American vintage. The low-lit homely space decorated with wooden fixtures and retro-phernalia is stocked to the eyeballs with old-school dapper ware such as fedoras, belts, leather loafers with tassels, and bow ties. You can find Steinbeck-era clothing – check shirts, bib tops, bandanas, overalls and waistcoats along with army-cool bomber jackets, boots and leather goods. The owner doubles as in-house tailor creating old-style new clothes and giving stock bespoke touches such as elbow patches.

6.

PATERSON, KINGSTON AND CLEVELAND STREETS
Causeway Bay
Open from 12pm

Hip young things with cash to spare will gravitate to this (relatively) quiet block, where malls give way to street-level shopping. Japanese fashion brands **Mercibeaucoup**, **Tsumori Chisato** and **Y3** differentiate this fashion hub from others in Hong Kong, as do lesser-franchised names like **A.P.C.**, **Gomme** and **Isabel Marant**. High-end names **Armani Exchange**, **Burberry** and **Max Mara** mingle with edgier **Zadig & Voltaire**, **Vivienne Westwood**, **Guess**, **Miss Sixty**, **Killah** and **Diesel**. There's the brand-heavy, good-looking European fashion house **Lusso Brillante** too. Cleveland Street is shoe central – check out **Camper**, **Shine**, **Religion** and, for true shoe eccentrics, Brit brand **Irregular Choice**.

TSUMORI CHISATO

7.

18 GRAMS

Unit C, 15 Cannon St,
Causeway Bay
2893 8988
www.18grams.com
Open Mon–Sun
8.30am–8.30pm

- -

Causeway Bay boasts one of the busiest pedestrian crossings in the world, a thoroughfare of bag-swagged shoppers marching between **Sogo** department store and Hysan Place (*see* p. 100). Not far away from the hustle and bustle, 18 Grams is a teeny-weeny corner establishment with just four tables, a tiny kitchen and a big-mumma espresso machine. The baristas here have no problems topping a latte with a fern frond, pet cat or love heart (if you're lucky). The food is simple, a cross between cha chaan teng (a Chinese rendition of Western food circa 1950s) and European. Hitting the spot on weekends is the big breakfast: snags, baked beans, eggs and a balsamic-dressed side salad.

8.

THE COFFEE ACADEMICS

38 Yiu Wa St, Causeway Bay
2156 0313
http://the-academics.com
Open Mon–Thurs 10am–11pm,
Fri–Sat 10am–2am,
Sun 12–9pm

Ever tried a latte sweetened with organic raw agave nectar and ground black pepper? This is the extreme coffee we're starting to see in a city traditionally all about tea. The Coffee Academics is well placed to experiment at large with coffee of all descriptions, including drip-ice varieties. The staunchly Hongkonger staff is verging on professional (a rare career path until recently) and dressed like they mean it (aprons, shirts, bow ties). The decor is both sumptuous and smart: lovely wood, metal and raw brickwork blend with dimly lit chandeliers, throw cushions and Tibetan fabrics. There's a selection of cakes and pastries, or order from a cafe menu with burritos, toasted sandwiches and the like.

9.

LITTLE BURRO
125 Leighton Rd, Causeway Bay
2336 3909
www.little-burro.com
Open Mon–Thurs & Sun 11am–
10pm, Fri–Sat 11am–11pm

During the Hong Kong Sevens rugby tournament (a party-cum-sporting-carnival held annually in March), Little Burro had the smarts to serve burritos from a stall outside its shop to hungry fans on their way to the stadium. Word spread quickly – this little shop with graffiti on its walls delivered on its promise of serving authentic San Francisco–style Mexican to the hungry hordes. Combinations include heavenly burritos filled with stringy pork or smoky chipotle chicken and topped with borracho beans, guacamole and corn green-chilli salsa. Tacos, salads and rice bowls hit the spot and go down a treat with Mexican Tecate bottled beer.

10.

DIN TAI FUNG

68 Yee Wo St, Causeway Bay
3160 8998
www.dintaifung.com.hk
Open Mon–Sun 11.30am–10pm

This heavenly dumpling joint from Taipei has gone global for a reason. An oversized glass window at the entry of DTF allows guests – local families and expats alike – to keep an eye on the kitchen, where a procession of hatted and scarved kitchen hands slavishly push and prod dumplings, before steaming them for exactly three minutes. They're on the table in seconds. If this doesn't whet your appetite, the menu will. Xiao long bao or soup dumplings are something of an art form here, with variations of the original pork version including crabmeat and black truffle. Don't mind the queues: the huge dining room and swift service mean you won't wait long. Green tea is poured on arrival, or order a beer.

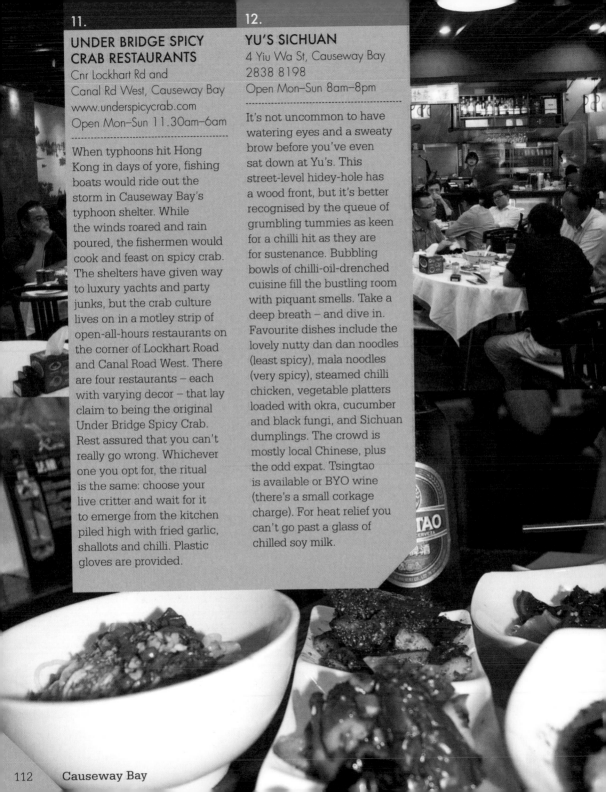

11.
UNDER BRIDGE SPICY CRAB RESTAURANTS
Cnr Lockhart Rd and
Canal Rd West, Causeway Bay
www.underspicycrab.com
Open Mon–Sun 11.30am–6am

When typhoons hit Hong Kong in days of yore, fishing boats would ride out the storm in Causeway Bay's typhoon shelter. While the winds roared and rain poured, the fishermen would cook and feast on spicy crab. The shelters have given way to luxury yachts and party junks, but the crab culture lives on in a motley strip of open-all-hours restaurants on the corner of Lockhart Road and Canal Road West. There are four restaurants – each with varying decor – that lay claim to being the original Under Bridge Spicy Crab. Rest assured that you can't really go wrong. Whichever one you opt for, the ritual is the same: choose your live critter and wait for it to emerge from the kitchen piled high with fried garlic, shallots and chilli. Plastic gloves are provided.

12.
YU'S SICHUAN
4 Yiu Wa St, Causeway Bay
2838 8198
Open Mon–Sun 8am–8pm

It's not uncommon to have watering eyes and a sweaty brow before you've even sat down at Yu's. This street-level hidey-hole has a wood front, but it's better recognised by the queue of grumbling tummies as keen for a chilli hit as they are for sustenance. Bubbling bowls of chilli-oil-drenched cuisine fill the bustling room with piquant smells. Take a deep breath – and dive in. Favourite dishes include the lovely nutty dan dan noodles (least spicy), mala noodles (very spicy), steamed chilli chicken, vegetable platters loaded with okra, cucumber and black fungi, and Sichuan dumplings. The crowd is mostly local Chinese, plus the odd expat. Tsingtao is available or BYO wine (there's a small corkage charge). For heat relief you can't go past a glass of chilled soy milk.

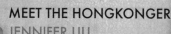

MEET THE HONGKONGER
JENNIFER LIU
ENTREPRENEUR

Jennifer Liu was born and raised in Hong Kong until age 12. During that time she fell in love with the style of coffee known as yuanyang, a milky concoction of black tea and Indonesian coffee. She came back to Hong Kong after the 1997 handover to China and in 2003 founded her first coffee establishment near Star Street in Wan Chai. It expanded into Hong Kong's first coffee academy in 2010, and in 2012 she developed the Coffee Academics (*see* p. 108).

How do you define Hong Kong's coffee scene?

It's really happening now, with neighbourhood cafes popping up everywhere. From handcrafted coffees to the latest state-of-the-art espresso machines, everyone is helping to create a unique coffee culture for Hong Kong.

What's your ideal day out?

Shopping in antique stores. I'd start at Teresa Coleman (*see* p. 026) and work my way up Hollywood Road popping into Arch Angel Antiques, Art Treasures Gallery and Yue Po Chai Antiques on the way (*see* map on p. 024). For eating and coffee I'd head to Café Gray Deluxe (*see* p. 060). Happy hour would be on Wyndham Street at the little French bar Pastis (*see* map on p. 025).

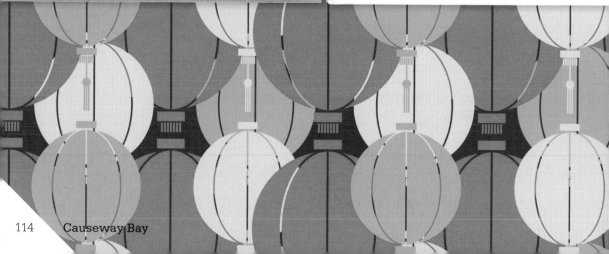

Where was the last great meal you had?

At Compass Room at the Royal Hong Kong Yacht Club in Causeway Bay. Dessert was particularly memorable: old-fashioned cherry jubilee (a cherry and liqueur dish) with flambéed crepe suzette.

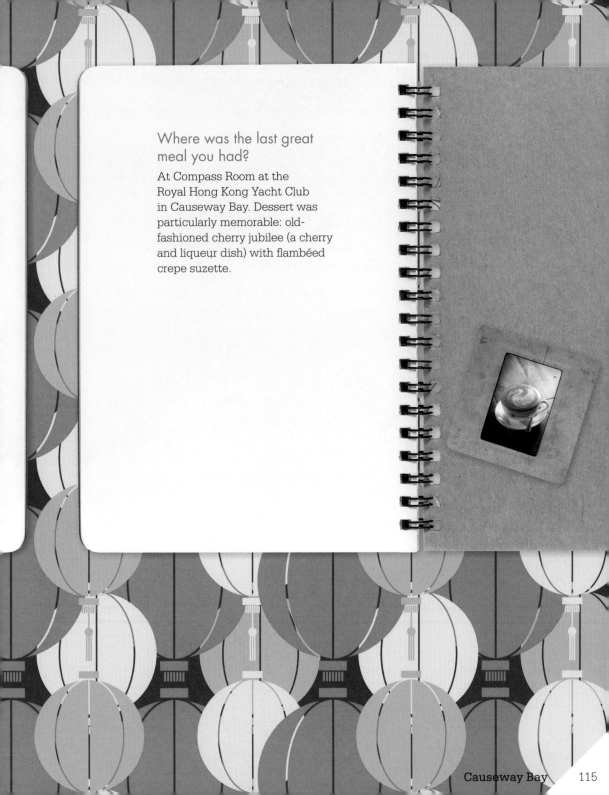

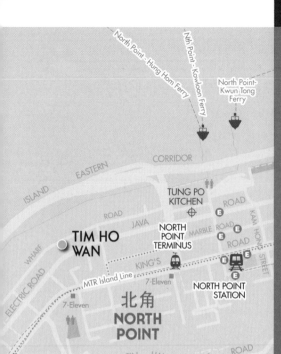

At the eastern end of Hong Kong Island, jutting into Kowloon Bay, these heavily urbanised neighbouring suburbs, with their own MTR stops, are slowly attracting outside attention. This is thanks mostly to major commercial endeavours such as the 68-storey One Island East skyscraper, and Taikoo Shing, a housing estate with a whopping 61 residential towers.

While it might not have much by way of traditional character, this is an eye-opening Hong Kong visual nevertheless. Off the main King's Road thoroughfare, you'll find a bit more street-level action with markets and shops offering a unique bo-peep into everyday Hong Kong life. Soho East is a relatively new waterside dining strip in nearby Sai Wan Ho.

North Point Station; Quarry Bay Station; Taikoo Station; Sai Wan Ho Station

ISLAND EAST – NORTH POINT, QUARRY BAY, TAIKOO AND SAI WAN HO

24   JUN 8016

SHOP AND EAT

1 ISLAND EAST MARKETS

17

EAT AND DRINK

2 SUGAR
3 PLAT DU JOUR
4 TAPEO
5 TIM HO WAN

VICTORIA   HARBOUR

MTR Tseung Kwan O Line

EASTERN

HARBOUR

CROSSING

ISLAND

EASTERN

CORRIDOR

TO
TIM HO WAN
(SEE MAP LEFT)

KING'S ROAD

HOI CHAK STREET

QUARRY BAY STATION

Ⓔ **TONG CHONG STREET**

Ⓔ

PLAT DU JOUR

Quarry Bay Park

Quarry Bay Park

TAPEO

Somerset House

ARTISTREE

ISLAND EAST MARKETS

Cornwall House

TAIKOO WAN

ROAD

太古城
TAIKOO SHING

Sai Wan Ho Playground

TAIKOO SHING ROAD

TAI FUNG AVENUE

7-Eleven

Cityplaza One

SUGAR

Hong Kong Film Archive

KING'S ROAD

Ⓔ KORNHILL ROAD

Hong Kong Tramways

MTR Island Line

7-Eleven

TAI KOO STATION

7-Eleven

HONG ON STREET

KING'S ROAD

鰂魚涌
QUARRY BAY

PARKER ROAD

GREIG ROAD

YUE STREET

STREET

HONG YUE STREET

HONG

STREET

YUE STREET

Ⓔ
SAI WAN HO STATION

QUARRY BAY

WALK

HONG SHING

HONG

YIU HING ROAD

LEI KING ROAD

TAI HONG STREET

MOUNT

WW II RUINS

WW II RUINS

0   200 m

WW II RUINS

Tai Tam Country Park (Quarry Bay Extension)

117

1.

ISLAND EAST MARKETS
Tong Chong St, Taikoo Pl,
Quarry Bay
2851 3220
www.islandeastmarkets.org
Open Sun 11am–5.30pm
(Sept–May)

- -

There's something surreal
about a farmers' market
sprouting in a concrete jungle,
but here's one that flourishes
despite its urban surrounds.
This first-rate addition to the
Hong Kong foodie scene is a
weekend hot spot for locals
stocking up on fresh organic
vegetables (plump tomatoes,
bunches of herbs, dirt-
encrusted root vegetables)
from farms in the New
Territories, creature comforts
(espresso-machine brewed
coffee, pastries and puffy
loaves of sourdough bread)
and crafts. Shoppers wanting
to tap into unique, homemade
and artisan products will find
clothes, quilts, shoes and
jewellery at reasonable prices.
Surrounding the market,
Tong Chong Street has a
smattering of restaurants.

2.

SUGAR

Level 32, East Hotel,
29 Taikoo Shing Rd, Taikoo
3968 3738
www.sugar-hongkong.com
Open Mon–Sat 5pm–2am,
Sun 12pm–12am

Back in the day, Kai Tak Airport sat in the middle of skyscraper suburbia and locals on their balconies could actually see passengers as the planes took off and landed. The airport has long since moved to Lantau Island, but the thrill of it can still be appreciated from Sugar, an open-air bar atop East Hotel with a view over the harbour and the former airport. The bar is party central and is therefore on the après-work radar of cashed-up financers working in nearby One Island East. Couches invite lounging around in the early evening, but resident DJ beats and pink-hued mood lighting amp up the atmosphere as the night goes on. New World and French wines wash well with stuffed jalapeño peppers and beer-battered prawns from the snack menu.

PLAT DU JOUR

21 Hoi Wan St, Quarry Bay
2789 4200
www.platdujourhk.com
Open Mon–Sun
11.30am–10.30pm

Hoi Wan Street, bisecting popular Tong Chong Street, looks set to be the next (or indeed the first) little hip-to-be-here Quarry Bay strip. Leading the pack, Plat du Jour is an ever-so-French bistro that can whisk you away from the surrounding high-rise metropolis to a Parisian street in an instant. Red leather booths, moody lighting and blackboard menus give it that European feel, but it's the French ingredients and produce that really shine. The perfect order: an elegant glass of sparkling Crémant d'Alsace; a perfectly formed quail yolk atop beef tartare; a slow-cooked pork chop with walnuts; a crème brûlée and cheeky 2005 sauterne.

4.

TAPEO

55 Tai Hong St, Sai Wan Ho
2513 0199
www.tapeo.hk
Open Mon–Sun 12pm–12am

Before Tapeo arrived, authentic Spanish food was not something Hong Kong did well. This upmarket Spanish bar, with an open front, lavish red bar stools and a share table with a view of the kitchen is the real deal. Pull up a pew, holler for a glass of cava (sparkling wine) and indulge in specialities – flown in weekly from southern Spain mind – such as jamón Ibérico (ham cured for 32 months and sliced directly off the bone), Iberian-style crispy pork belly, stuffed piquillo peppers and crab tortilla. Vegetarian offerings such as patatas bravas (fried potatoes with a spicy tomato sauce) and pan con tomate (toasted bread with tomato, garlic, olive oil and salt) are straight from the tapas bars of Andalusia. If you miss out on a seat, the waterside promenade that Tapeo is on – dubbed **Soho East** – also has a handful of other eateries.

5.

TIM HO WAN

Seaview Building,
2–8 Wharf Rd, North Point
2979 5608
Open Mon–Sun 10am–9.30pm

When Tim Ho Wan in Mong Kok earned a Michelin star, the dim sum offerings became the cheapest Michelin-starred dishes in the world. The restaurant closed down after a rent hike but offshoots of the original still offer awesome cheap-arse dumplings, albeit minus the star. This North Point incarnation in a low-profile street of residential high-rises is far bigger than the original. The local grey-haired contingent, which lines up just before 10am to bag a seat, is a good indication of decent grub. Inside it is as unfussy as it is fun, with a lot of cutlery clatter and chitter-chatter adding to the experience. Order the regulars – pork buns, har gow (shrimp dumplings) and siu mai (pork dumplings) – or get adventurous with cheong fun (rice noodle rolls), homemade cuttlefish balls and turnip cakes.

4.

5.

HOT TIP
One Island East is home
to the ArtisTree art space
(see map on p. 117),
which hosts excellent
artists and exhibitions.
Grab a local guide for
current events.

os Peq
Oil

ed Olives

e & Honey $65

nchovies $65

$65

88

$98

$98

Class
傳統

Cho
西班

Mus
紅椒

Cra
西班

S

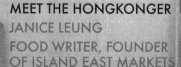

MEET THE HONGKONGER
JANICE LEUNG
FOOD WRITER, FOUNDER OF ISLAND EAST MARKETS

Hong Kong–born, Aussie–Hong Kong bred Janice Leung has always straddled two countries and cultures. This hybridity ignited her passion for food and eventually food writing. This, in turn, led to her founding Island East Markets (*see* p. 118), which aims to make shopping for local produce a habit.

How do you define Hong Kong's cuisine?

It's primarily Cantonese, with pockets of Hakka, Chiuchow and Shanghainese. Some food traditions are truly Hongkongese, such as our cha chaan tengs, which are Hong Kong–style diners serving milk tea, egg tarts, toast with condensed milk and macaroni in soup with luncheon meat (spam). They're an offshoot of European and American influences. Recently, Hong Kong has seen a lot of restaurants, cafes and bars focused on artisan ingredients and methods, like the use of sous-vide machines at Kin's Kitchen in Wan Chai, known for its classic (and often laborious) Cantonese food.

What are your favourite Hong Kong eating venues?

Some places like Wan Chai's Seventh Son respect the natural flavours of well-sourced ingredients. I can't get

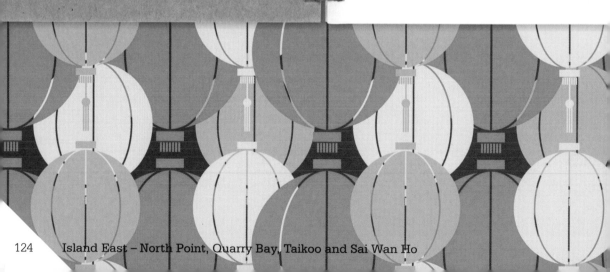

enough of its scrambled eggs with prawns. I also love cha chaan tengs, especially For Kee in Sheung Wan (*see* map on p. 126) for its milk tea and fried rice with pork chops, and Hoi On cafe,, also in Sheung Wan (*see* map on p. 127) for its retro charm and 'French' toast. Wan Chai's Sang Kee is a home-style Cantonese stalwart and Zhe Jiang Heen is a Shanghainese favourite. Amber, at the Landmark Mandarin Oriental (*see* map on p. 001) in Central, was the first truly world-class modern European restaurant in Hong Kong.

Where do you escape to when the city gets too much?

Remote Sai Kung in the New Territories. The beaches and hikes there are beautiful – chances are, you'll have a beach to yourself.

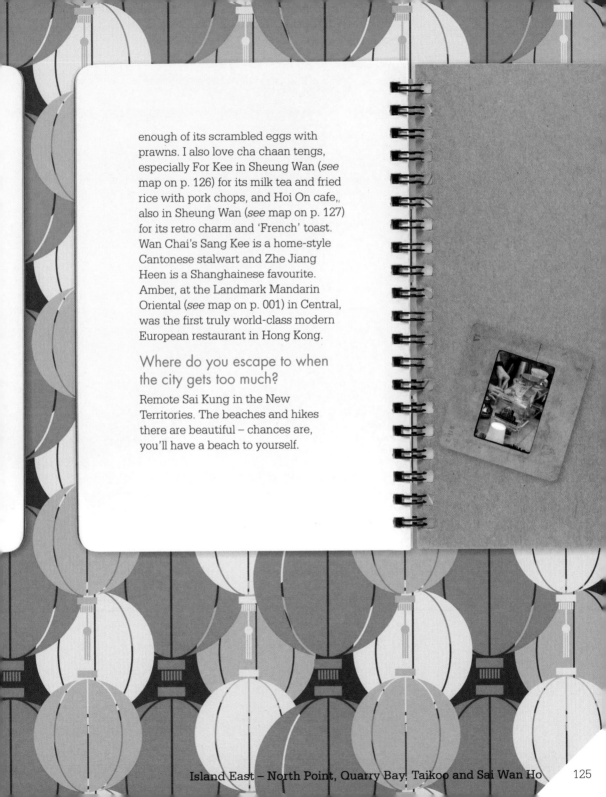

Map labels

MTR Island Line

TO DRIED SEAFOOD STREET

ABC KITCHEN

WING

LOK

BONHAM STRAND

QUEEN STREET

STREET

ROAD

QUEEN'S

WEST

STREET

WEST

DEEM

Hollywood Road Park

HOLLYWOOD ROAD

LOMOGRAPHY

POSSESSION

WA LANE

208 DUECENTO OTTO

CHACHAWAN

FOR KEE

LITTLE BURRO

PO YAN STREET

KWONG FOOK I TSZ (PAK SHING TEMPLE)

NOSH

SIN SIN

SAI STREET

WATER

LANE

PO HING FONG

Blake Garden

MOOD

TEAKHA

TAI PING SHAN

YUK KIN

IN BETWEEN

SHEUNG WAN

SHEUNG WAN

Once the dead end of town, Sheung Wan on Hong Kong Island has stepped into the it-right-now limelight. In the process of avoiding Central's exorbitant rents, Manhattan-worthy bars and restaurants, artisan shops and design studios have created a hands-down better alternative. For the hipsters in Hong Kong, this is party headquarters.

Adding to the intrigue, the precinct's mess of steeply sloping roads and cobbled laneways are home to pockets of low-rise terraces, vertiginous residential blocks, temples and colonial buildings. It's a great place to get lost. If you have time, keep walking beyond Sheung Wan into Sai Ying Pun, which has similar charm and is touted as the next hip hot spot.

Sheung Wan Station

---

24   JUN 8016

SHOP

1 CHINESE MEDICINE AND DRIED SEAFOOD STREETS
2 DEEM
3 SELECT-18
4 PETIT BAZAAR
5 SQUARE STREET
6 UPPER LASCAR ROW (AKA CAT STREET)

17

SHOP, EAT AND DRINK

7 GOUGH STREET
8 TAI PING SHAN

EAT

9 BARISTA JAM

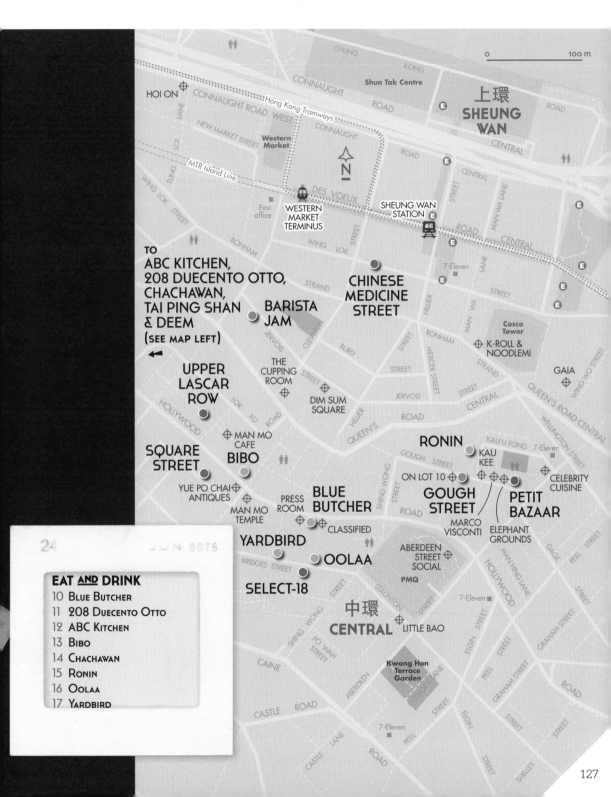

0   100 m

Shun Tak Centre

CONNAUGHT

KONG

ROAD

上環
SHEUNG
WAN

HOI ON
CONNAUGHT ROAD WEST

Hong Kong Tramways

CONNAUGHT

ROAD

CENTRAL

NEW MARKET STREET

Western
Market

WING LOK STREET

LOI

TUNG

MTR Island Line

CENTRAL

DES VOEUX

N

Post
office

WESTERN
MARKET
TERMINUS

SHEUNG WAN
STATION

ROAD

CENTRAL

BONHAM

WING

LOK

7-Eleven

TO
ABC KITCHEN,
208 DUECENTO OTTO,
CHACHAWAN,
TAI PING SHAN
& DEEM
(SEE MAP LEFT)

STRAND

BARISTA
JAM

CHINESE
MEDICINE
STREET

HILLIER

BONHAM

STREET

STREET

MAN WA LANE

Cosco
Tower

MAN WO STREET

K-ROLL &
NOODLEMI

GAIA

UPPER
LASCAR
ROW

THE
CUPPING
ROOM

JERVOIS

CLEVERLY

BURD

STREET

MERCER STREET

STRAND

QUEEN'S ROAD CENTRAL

WELLINGTON STREET

HOLLYWOOD

LOK

KU

ROAD

DIM SUM
SQUARE

STREET

HILLIER

JERVOIS

ROAD

CENTRAL

RONIN

KAU U FONG

7-Eleven

MAN MO
CAFE

QUEEN'S

ROAD

KAU
KEE

SQUARE
STREET

BIBO

GOUGH

STREET

ON LOT 10

PETIT
BAZAAR

CELEBRITY
CUISINE

GAGE

YUE PO CHAI
ANTIQUES

MAN MO
TEMPLE

PRESS
ROOM

BLUE
BUTCHER

SHING WONG

ROAD

GOUGH
STREET

MARCO
VISCONTI

ELEPHANT
GROUNDS

MAN HING LANE

YARDBIRD

CLASSIFIED

ABERDEEN
STREET
SOCIAL

HOLLYWOOD

PEEL

GRAHAM STREET

BRIDGES STREET

OOLAA

STAUNTON

PMQ

7-Eleven

GRAHAM STREET

SELECT-18

SHING WONG

PO WAH
STREET

中環
CENTRAL

LITTLE BAO

ELGIN

ELGIN

STREET

STREET

CAINE

Kwong Hon
Terrace
Garden

ABERDEEN

GRAHAM

ROAD

CASTLE

ROAD

LANE

7-Eleven

PEEL

STREET

SHELLEY

24

JUN 8DT6

1.

CHINESE MEDICINE AND DRIED SEAFOOD STREETS

Wing Lok St and Des Voeux Rd
West, Sheung Wan
Open Mon–Sun 9.30am–7pm

Deer antlers, skeletal
seahorses, sea cucumbers and
an Alice in Wonderland–esque
selection of dried mushrooms
overflow from baskets
outside shopfronts on Wing
Lok Street, the heart of the
traditional Chinese medicine
trade. On nearby Des Voeux
Road West, the potent smell
of salted and dried fish and
seafood fills the air. This is the
place for traditional Chinese
produce such as black moss,
dried sausage, and, dare we
say it, shark fin and abalone.
The scene here is lovingly
local with housewives doing
their shopping and old men
talking shop. Photo-tastic.

DEEM
252 Hollywood Rd,
Sheung Wan
2540 2011
http://deemlimited.com
Open Mon–Sat 12–7pm,
Sun 1–6pm

Is it possible to covet everything in a shop? Yes. Deem is a wonderfully warm interior-design store with high ceilings, terrazzo floors and a homely vintage colour palette. Owner Debra Little has seamlessly blended original mid-20th-century vintage furniture – Compass dining chairs and an Eames chaise longue for example – with exquisite art and ornaments, much of which is designed in-house. There are hand-beaten brass trays, planters and vases, made-to-order plush velvet sofas and leather ottomans, handcrafted pottery, ceramics and stoneware along with hand-loomed wool throws and damask carpets. Equally distinctive is Little's collection of modernist Scandinavian jewellery.

3.

SELECT-18

18 Bridges St, Sheung Wan
9127 3657
Open Mon–Wed 12–9pm,
Thurs–Sat 12–11pm,
Sun 12–8pm

Thomas Lee, the owner of this one-off ode to vintage cool, has a knack for dusting away the cobwebs to showcase bygone fashion staples in a sparkling new light. Step inside to see coathangers shrouded in old furs, racks of dresses and skirts, dishevelled mannequin torsos dripping with beads and well-loved shoes cluttering the tiled floor. On tables crowded with earrings, sunglasses, wallets and bags, the odd home-decor item gets a look-in: typewriters, cameras, telephones, televisions, lamps and clocks. Aside from the occasional tweed cap, this place mostly caters to the gals, or the gals in your life. And don't expect too much competition – Hongkongers are still warming to the second-hand trend.

4.

PETIT BAZAAR

9 Gough St, Sheung Wan
2544 2255
www.petit-bazaar.com
Open Mon–Sun 10am–8pm

Children's store Petit Bazaar was one of the first shops to move into Gough Street before it became ubercool. Its ongoing success is due to a simple philosophy: it sells beautiful quality French furniture, toys, games, clothing and bedroom decor in a magical fairytale environment. Baby-squirrel night lights and brightly coloured rugs decorate the floor, paper lampshades hang from the ceiling and shelves are packed with imaginative toys and games – marbles, balls, beads, blocks and crocheted knick-knacks to name just a few. You'll find reasonably priced leather handbags and baby essentials too. The **Wan Chai branch** (*see* map on p. 065) also has kids' kitchenware, such as designer melamine plates and cups.

4.

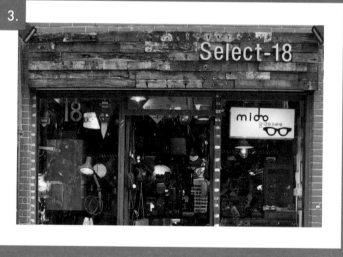

Select-18

4.

4.

3.

5.

SQUARE STREET

15 Square St, Sheung Wan
2362 1086
www.squarestreet.se
Open Mon–Sun 11am–7pm

Created in 2010 by Swedish design duo Alexis Holm and David Ericsson, Square Street is a neat little boutique for both men and women that manages to perfect sartorial Scandinavian designs. Holm's footwear and Ericsson's Void Watches are what people come for, but the shop, an artisan's hidey-hole with shoeboxes reaching the ceiling, has worthy impulse purchases, including hand-crafted leather wallets, satchels and handbags. While you're here take a look around Square Street – the street. Holm and Ericsson moved in and the bearded brigade followed, turning this area into a den of creativity.

UPPER LASCAR ROW (AKA CAT STREET)
Sheung Wan

A Mao tote bag from
G.O.D. (*see* p. 176) is a
more representative Hong
Kong souvenir these days,
but traditionalists looking
for old-world accessories
and artefacts will love the
Upper Lascar Row (or Cat
Street market). Found just
off Hollywood Road, this
pedestrian-only lane and
the surrounding streets are
a hub for antique stores,
art galleries, curio shops
and hawker stalls selling
everything from ancient snuff
bottles and Mao cigarette
lighters to jade bangles and
Ming vases. If you're looking
for real antiques, sidestep
the street stalls. That dusty
box of treasures sitting
on the footpath is more
likely to be off a mainland
factory floor than from the
Forbidden City.

7.

GOUGH STREET
Sheung Wan
Open Mon–Sun from 11am

Once the printing sector of Sheung Wan, Gough Street has gone from gritty to groovy in the space of five years. Head here for disposable-income shopping, and be sure to explore the little side streets too. Funky furniture shops include another branch of Homeless (*see* p. 100), **Mr Blacksmith** and king of cool Britannia **Timothy Oulton**. For fashion, pop by **Marco Visconti** and **Cheap Monday**. There's a Petit Bazaar (*see* p. 130) here, and **Elephant Grounds** for coffee. **On Lot 10**, where Cantonese cuisine meets French fusion, is a super dinner venue, but for awesome beef-brisket noodles, you'll love **Kau Kee**, which still has formica tables, plastic awnings and endless lunchtime queues.

HOMELESS

TAI PING SHAN
Sheung Wan
Open Mon–Sun from 3pm

- -

One of Hong Kong's oldest neighbourhoods is now its hottest property. Tai Ping Shan, a street with a mix of edgy and ancient, is the pedestrianised backbone of a chilled little area where art galleries, independent start-ups and cafes have opened.

The hit list: **Nosh** serves lunches prepped with fresh ingredients, **Yuk Kin** does wicked fried rice, and masala chai is a favourite at homely **Teakha**. **In Between** sells antiques and collectibles with a hint of pop culture, and **Mood** is a barbershop-cum-purveyor-of-menswear. **Para Site** is an artist-run gallery on nearby Po Yan Street. Next door, **Lomography** deals in iconic analog Lomo cameras. Unless you're coming for lunch, don't bother rocking up before 3pm – most shops open in their own time.

9.

BARISTA JAM
126–128 Jervois St,
Sheung Wan
2854 2211
www.baristajam.com.hk
Open Mon & Sat 10am–6pm,
Tues–Fri 8am–6pm

The boys from Barista Jam
are known enviably for their
heavy artillery, aka their
expensive coffee machines,
proof of a serious coffee
addiction. Barista Jam was
one of the first authentic
coffee places in Hong Kong
and remains one of the
coolest. The small concrete
bunker on chaotic Jervois
Street has tables with just
enough room to spread a
paper (or tap on an iPad),
and a sleek coffee counter
for downing a macchiato,
Italian style. Food-on-the-go
includes pastries, toasties
and sandwiches – or stay
awhile for smoked-salmon
pasta followed by crème
brûlée. The Japanese ice-drip
coffee and background jazz
top off the experience.

10.

BLUE BUTCHER
108 Hollywood Rd,
Sheung Wan
2613 9286
www.bluebutcher.com
Open Mon–Sun 12am–12pm

If animal protein is not
your thing, look away now.
Blue Butcher is the city's
hippest meat house, where
moneyed meat lovers go to
look good chowing down
on some of the world's best
cuts. There's a cocktail bar at
street level or head upstairs
to the warehouse space with
its earthy toned Manhattan
makeover – leather-topped
stools, parquet floors, wooden
chairs and marble tabletops.
The menu is carnivorously
good. Try bone marrow, toast
and caper berries or Dutch
veal cheek and sweetbreads.
For drinks, a Horse's Head
has horseradish-infused gin,
while a Bangers and Mash
is bacon-washed vodka and
sweet-potato syrup.

11.

208 DUECENTO OTTO

208 Hollywood Rd,
Sheung Wan
2549 0208
www.208.com.hk
Open Mon–Sat 12pm–12am,
Sun 10am–10pm

- -

Duecento Otto was one of the early comers to Sheung Wan, bringing with it a New York Meatpacking–district vibe inspired by the two-storey building's former life as a meat warehouse. Here, industrial steel meets wood-crafted ceilings and floors, and European tiles with Chinese motifs. It's a combo that pulls a crowd. Downstairs is abuzz with aperitivi drinkers sipping on apricot bellinis (sparkling wine mixed with fresh juice) and diners perched casually at high tables indulging in quattro funghi pizzas, salumi (cured meat) platters and burrata cheese flown in fresh from Italia. Upstairs is more intimate, with rustic Italian dishes, such as braised-veal osso buco with saffron risotto, and a Euro-centric wine list with 20 varieties of wine by the glass.

ABC KITCHEN

Shop CF7, Food Market,
1 Queen St, Sheung Wan
9278 8227
www.abckitchen.com.hk
Open Mon–Sat 12–2.30pm &
7–10.30pm, Sun 7–10.30pm

A few years back, popular Hong Kong restaurant M at the Fringe, sister restaurant to Shanghai's famed M on the Bund, closed down. Its long-term kitchen staff, now adept at Australian-style European cuisine, obscurely set up shop in a Sheung Wan wet market. And it's a hit. ABC Kitchen serves gourmand food on chequered tablecloths amid a Cantonese and noodle trade elsewhere in the market. The logo is Italian but the fare is European, from duck confit and linguine vongole (clams) to foie gras and eye fillet. It also serves the best pavlova around. Bookings for this most excellent cross-cultural culinary enigma are recommended.

13.

BIBO
163 Hollywood Rd,
Sheung Wan
2956 3188
www.bibo.hk
Open Mon–Sat 12–2.30pm &
5pm–12am, Sun 11am–4pm &
5pm–12am

A discreet gold door? A tuxedoed doorman? Is this *Twin Peaks*? No, this is Bibo, an outlandishly extravagant French restaurant where contemporary fine dining meets, wait for it, street art. The serious line-up of contemporary artworks in situ – by Banksy, Jean-Michel Basquiat, Damien Hirst, Daniel Arsham, Jeff Koons and Hong Kong's own King of Kowloon (aka Tsang Tsou Choi) – make it necessary viewing. The art is set against Prussian-blue furnishings and tiles, brass pipes and French-oak floors. Foie gras coupled with grenadine-poached rhubarb, and seared scallops served with corn-and-herb pistou (like pesto) are culinary works of art. Finish with a rare cognac by the fireplace, among books about Basquiat, et al. It's no boho Paris, but it's pretty special.

HOT TIP

Not far from Upper Lascar Row (*see* p. 133), take a peek at Man Mo Temple, built in 1847. It pays tribute to two deities: Literature (Man) and War (Mo). Man Mo Cafe (*see* map on p. 127) on Upper Lascar Row does decent dim sum. You'll also get a sneak peak through the restaurant window into Bibo (*see* opposite page), which is disguised as the French Tramway Co that originally stood here.

14.

CHACHAWAN
206 Hollywood Rd,
Sheung Wan
2549 0020
www.chachawan.hk
Open Mon–Sun 12–3pm &
5.30pm–12am

Prepare to tuck into the sweet-salt-sour-heat sensation that is Isaan Thai, a cuisine from Thailand's north-east. The grilled-meat dishes here are especially good and are best shared. Try the marinated chicken thigh, grilled till crispy and served with chilli sauce. The whole tiger prawns are smothered in dry red coconut curry and fresh lime, and fire-grilled (goong golae). Wooden stools, a mosaic-tiled floor and Thai illustrations layered on vintage Hong Kong posters add to the good-fun vibe. There's a no-reservations policy, which might mean sitting around drinking lemongrass caipirinha cocktails until a table comes up. Such is life.

RONIN

8 On Wo La, Sheung Wan
2547 5263
www.roninhk.com
Open Mon–Sat 6pm–12am

With only 14 leather-clad bar seats and the rest standing room, Ronin is fiercely difficult to get into. That said, this curious little Japanese joint, hidden behind an unsigned door, is worth the effort. These guys, the Yardbird dudes (*see* p. 145), know food, people and Japan and have pooled their knowledge to awesome effect. Nippon whisky, sake and beer, playful Japanese cooking techniques and a rare casual ambience give the place a heartbeat that's hard to beat. A tasting menu might include yellowtail sashimi, crispy deep-fried scallops, flower crab mixed with mitsuba (a Japanese herb similar to parsley) and creamy uni (sea urchin), and carpaccio Kagoshima beef with maitake mushrooms and a raw egg. It's all delicious. On Wo Lane is off Gough Street (*see* p. 134).

16.

OOLAA

Bridges St, Sheung Wan
2803 2083
www.casteloconcepts.com
Open Mon–Sun 7am–late

The sister establishment to Wagyu (*see* p. 031), Oolaa, with its wood furniture, tiled floor and elongated central bar, is a hive of casual activity, be it for early breakfast, lunch, dinner or drinks. In the mornings, the open-fronted cafe with couches and low-slung coffee tables is the domain of lycra-clad diners (fresh from a walk on Victoria Peak) sipping lattes and eating eggs Benedict. At lunch, the central share tables attract well-heeled punters enjoying antipodean wines and antipasti. Dinner is slightly more formal, with big groups occupying white-linen-covered tables and dining on eye-fillet steaks, Thai beef salads, fajitas and thin-crust pizzas.

YARDBIRD

33–35 Bridges St, Sheung Wan
2547 9273
www.yardbirdrestaurant.com
Open Mon–Sat 6pm–12am

Yardbird is up there with Hong Kong's hottest. When it opened in 2011, it revolutionised the dining scene, bringing with it a kind of Japanese-influenced New York style of dining that kowtowed to kick-arse food, rocking cocktails and a graffiti aesthetic. It serves yakitori (food grilled on skewers) with a heavy leaning towards chicken (thigh, breast, wings, neck). But the hands-down best dishes are out of left field: the KFC (Korean fried cauliflower) and Yardbird Caesar, for example. Wash your meal down with a sake, Japanese pale ale or Bloody Kim Jong-il cocktail (vodka, kimchi and tomato). There is no service charge, and reservations aren't taken.

MEET THE HONGKONGER
ALAN LO
RESTAURATEUR, ENTREPRENEUR

Alan Lo co-founded Hong Kong Ambassadors of Design in 2006 when the city's creative and cultural development was still in its infancy. Around the same time he opened the Press Room and Classified restaurants in Sheung Wan (*see* map on p. 127). Since then, Sheung Wan has become the unofficial creative hub for foreign design studios and local creative talent. One restaurant project led to another and today Lo operates in 14 locations across the city.

What's trending in design in Hong Kong?

Anything small and artisanal. The city currently favours things by young passionate entrepreneurs in interesting up-and-coming neighbourhoods like Sai Ying Pun, between Kennedy Town and Sheung Wan, and Sham Shui Po in Kowloon.

What is your favourite heritage area?

Third Street in Sai Ying Pun retains a lot of Hong Kong's original charm, with traditional street-level shops and local restaurants. Although the neighbourhood is changing, Third Street evokes a sense of history and authenticity.

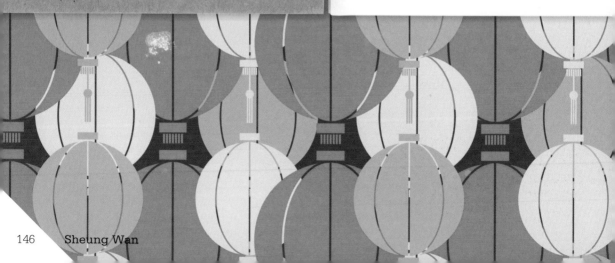

Where was your last great meal?

At Amber at the Landmark Mandarin Oriental in Central (*see* map on p. 001). Aside from the impeccable service and relaxed setting, the food is always inventive, consistent and beautifully presented.

Where do you go for a glass of fine wine?

Aberdeen Street Social at PMQ (*see* p. 039). Be sure to ask head sommelier Fergus Muirhead for his personal recommendation.

You can still see red plastic lampshades swinging in the fruit and veg shops here, and hardware stores packed with stuff direct from mainland factories, but this Hong Kong Island waterside pocket is nevertheless on the road to gentrification. The completion of the extended Island Line will soon give Kennedy Town its own MTR station, and property prices have gone up accordingly.

The emergence of funky eateries such as Sunday's Grocery (*see* p. 154) and Fish & Chick (*see* p. 152) indicates that expats are infiltrating what has up until now been a very local neighbourhood. Make tracks for Davis Street and the New Praya promenade-of-sorts, if not for sand, then at least some ocean spray. The view is something else too – industry layered with natural beauty (or have I been in Hong Kong too long?).

BELCHER BAY

KENNEDY TOWN NEW PRAYA

CADOGAN STREET

The Merton

24   JUN 8016

EAT AND DRINK

1   Bistro du Vin
2   Fish & Chick
3   Piccolo Pizzeria & Bar
4   Sunday's Grocery

KENNEDY TOWN

BELCHER BAY

N

KENNEDY TOWN NEW PRAYA

Kennedy
Town
Fire
Station

FISH &
CHICK

BULLDOGS

HARBOUR
RESTAURANT

Hing Wong
Building

SMITHFIELD

DAVIS

Grand
Fortune
Mansion

Manhattan
Heights

Ka On
Building

Ka Fu
Building

May Sun
Building

BISTRO
DU VIN

The Merton

PICCOLO
PIZZERIA
& BAR

STREET

STREET

CATCHICK

0   50 m

DAVIS

SUNDAY'S
GROCERY

STREET

The Merton

HAU WO

堅尼地城
KENNEDY TOWN

STREET

STREET

STREET

BELCHER'S

BELCHER'S STREET

Luen Yau
Apartments

Luen Hong
Apartments

1.

BISTRO DU VIN
1 Davis St, Kennedy Town
2824 3010
www.facebook.com/
bistroduvin.hk
Open Mon & Wed–Sun
12–2pm & 6–10pm,
Tues 6–10pm

Two French bistros stand side by side here, but locals tend to give this one the thumbs up, perhaps because it's the least formal. Bistro du Vin is a warm and cosy cavern with a mosaic tiled floor, exposed brick walls, timber panels and bottles of vino reaching to the ceiling. It's packed at lunch with diners indulging in bouillabaisse and coq au vin served in heavy colourful casserole dishes, and is similarly popular for dinner, when it's best to book. Any French person worth their blue, white and red will be impressed by the gravity-defying Grand Marnier soufflé. Burgundy, Beaujolais and syrah dot the French wine list.

2.

FISH & CHICK

Shop 6, 25 New Praya,
Kennedy Town
2974 0088
www.facebook.com/
fishandchick
Open Sun–Thurs 12–10pm,
Fri–Sat 12–11pm

Give it a few years, and the industrial waterfront strip called **New Praya** will be a lively landscaped promenade. Despite its current raw appeal, the sunset view remains one of the best on Hong Kong Island. Fish & Chick is the brightest shop on the strip, with an open-fronted upmarket 'chippy' daubed in bright yellow and blue with a maritime theme. Co-founder Paul, who spent his university days in Australia, delivers classy Aussie-style fish and chips with crispy-crunchy batter and eye-popping green mushy peas, along with fresh caesar and smoked-salmon salads. The smallish roast chickens are market-fresh and marinated, so they're deliciously tender. There's red and white house wine by the glass and beer on tap. Happy days.

3.

PICCOLO PIZZERIA & BAR

Shop 1E, Davis St,
Kennedy Town
2824 3000
www.facebook.com/piccolokt
Open Mon 6pm–12am,
Tues–Sun 11.30am–12am

The smell of dough crisping in a wood-fired oven wafts around this casual cosmopolitan pizzeria, kitted out with a bar, tiled flooring, bench seats, and high tables and stools. Roman-style thin-based pizzas are the speciality on a menu that favours good old-fashioned flavours and seasonal ingredients. The pizza pancetta with bacon and tomato sauce topped with a freshly cracked egg is a good example. Pasta dishes include aglio e olio, with roasted garlic, red chilli and olive oil, and nduja de Calabria (live prawns tossed with salami and chilli). Bigger appetites should try the wild-caught white fish baked in white-wine sauce with clams, cherry tomatoes, potatoes and garlic.

4.

SUNDAY'S GROCERY

66–68 Catchick St,
Kennedy Town
2628 6001
www.sundaysgrocery.com
Open Tues–Sun 12–9pm

- -

Acrylic, neon, metal and hand-painted futuristic signage delivers a stylised cartoonish quality to this fantastically cool grocery store – it's a joy to behold. In addition to the best pulled-pork and coleslaw sandwiches on the island, its shelves are chockers with a line-up of produce that a quality snob can't go past. Groceries run along the lines of iced tea, spices from sister restaurant Yardbird (*see* p. 145) and tomato sauce bottles you just don't see in supermarkets. In terms of alcoholic offerings, you'll see sake, Japanese whisky, shochu (a distilled Japanese beverage), beer and small-batch spirits alongside wine. Fried chicken is served every Sunday, and – ever the design gurus – it comes packaged in the store's own paper.

WELCOME

HOT TIP
In nearby Sai Ying Pun, Ping Pong 129 is an old table-tennis hall recently turned into a high-spirited Spanish gin bar.

American Yvonne Cheung has been visiting Hong Kong since she was a kid, but it wasn't until 2010 that she packed her bags and moved to Hong Kong to work as a wine guru at Café Gray Deluxe (*see* p. 060). She and her partner, one of the peeps behind Yardbird (*see* p. 145) and Ronin (*see* p. 143), have made Kennedy Town their home.

Where do you like to eat and drink in Kennedy Town?

It's a fantastic place, with so many new shops and restaurants. I'm a sucker for Fish & Chick (*see* p. 152), a waterside restaurant with the best fish and chips and roast chicken! Next door is Bulldogs (*see* map on p. 149), always playing my favourite tunes from the '90s (dating myself, I know), and great for some sliders. Harbour Restaurant (*see* map on p. 149), on the same strip, has uberdelicious Cantonese fare, and further around the corner is Bistro du Vin (*see* p. 150), where the food is always thoughtful, and corkage always free! Sunday's Grocery (*see* p. 154), a quirky little liquor-cum-grocery store, has some of the best sandwiches – schnitzel, falafel, chicken meatball ...

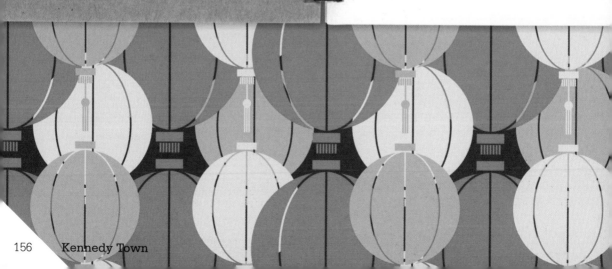

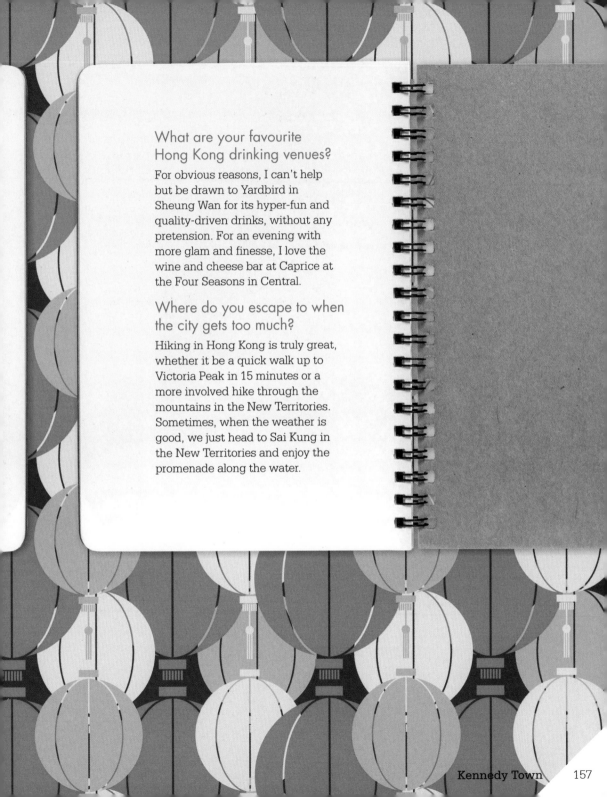

What are your favourite Hong Kong drinking venues?

For obvious reasons, I can't help but be drawn to Yardbird in Sheung Wan for its hyper-fun and quality-driven drinks, without any pretension. For an evening with more glam and finesse, I love the wine and cheese bar at Caprice at the Four Seasons in Central.

Where do you escape to when the city gets too much?

Hiking in Hong Kong is truly great, whether it be a quick walk up to Victoria Peak in 15 minutes or a more involved hike through the mountains in the New Territories. Sometimes, when the weather is good, we just head to Sai Kung in the New Territories and enjoy the promenade along the water.

薄扶林
POK FU LAM

HONG KONG TRAIL

TIN WAN HILL ROAD

SHEK PAI WAN ROAD

McDonald's
7-Eleven
7-Eleven

TIN WAN PRAYA ROAD

KAI LUNG WAN

Aberdeen – Yung Shue Wan Ferry

Aberdeen – Sok Kwu Wan Ferry

STH HORIZONS DR
7-Eleven
Starbucks

ABERDEEN

On the southern side of Hong Kong Island, broad, sweeping Aberdeen incorporates Aberdeen Harbour, Wong Chuk Hang and Ap Lei Chau, a road-accessed island. The harbour, overlooked by dozens of same-same residential towers, is home to Jumbo (*see* p. 168) and a flotilla of brilliant sampan fishing boats. Away from the water, the area is OTT urbanised, a concrete enclave that is slowly becoming more interesting.

In the industrial warehouses stacked either side of double-decker Wong Chuk Hang Road, unexpected boutiques have set up shop. On nearby Ap Lei Chau, pin-thin Horizon Plaza (*see* p. 161) is a Chinese shopping experience that shouldn't be missed.

24   JUN 8076

SHOP
1. BOWERBIRD
2. HORIZON PLAZA
3. CASA CAPRIZ
4. ED1TUS
5. MIRTH

17

SHOP AND EAT
6. TREE

EAT AND DRINK
7. JUMBO
8. THE BUTCHERS CLUB DELI

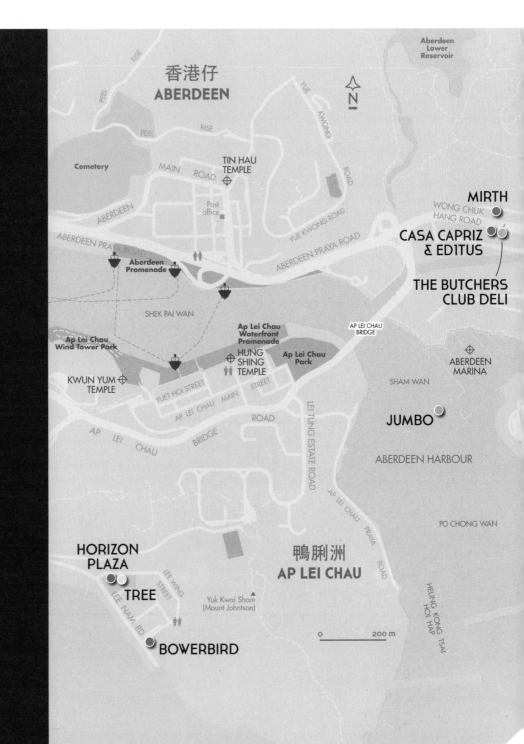

香港仔
ABERDEEN

Aberdeen
Lower
Reservoir

Cemetery

**TIN HAU
TEMPLE**

MIRTH
WONG CHUK
HANG ROAD

**CASA CAPRIZ
& EDITUS**

Post
office

**THE BUTCHERS
CLUB DELI**

ABERDEEN PRAYA ROAD

Aberdeen
Promenade

ABERDEEN PRAYA ROAD

SHEK PAI WAN

AP LEI CHAU
BRIDGE

Ap Lei Chau
Waterfront
Promenade

ABERDEEN
MARINA

Ap Lei Chau
Wind Tower Park

Ap Lei Chau
Park

SHAM WAN

**HUNG
SHING
TEMPLE**

KWUN YUM
TEMPLE

YUET HOI STREET

JUMBO

AP LEI CHAU MAIN STREET

ABERDEEN HARBOUR

AP LEI CHAU   BRIDGE   ROAD

LEI TUNG ESTATE ROAD

PO CHONG WAN

**HORIZON
PLAZA**

鴨脷洲
AP LEI CHAU

LEE WING STREET

TREE

LEE NAM RD

Yuk Kwai Sham
(Mount Johntson)

0   200 m

BOWERBIRD

1.

BOWERBIRD

Unit 5, Level 2, 2 Lee Lok St,
Ap Lei Chau, Aberdeen
2552 2727
www.bowerbird-home.com
Open Mon–Sun 10am–6pm

In this fantastically random
10,000-square-foot warehouse,
Australian-born, Hong Kong–
based Philippa Haydon has
evolved her fondness for
blue-and-white Chinoiserie
ceramics into a full-blown
business. Bowerbird is a
wholesaler but also sells
direct to the public, with
global shipping available.
While much of the furniture
is sourced from New York
and Paris, Asian-accented
treasures have been artfully
incorporated so as to blend
in with Western-style
interiors. Big-ticket items
include armoires, bedside
tables, dining chairs and
rattan and wicker baskets.
Luggage-sized pieces include
hand-painted ceramic
ginger jars, pots and vases.
The freestanding Chinese
birdcages filled with scented
candles and exquisite hand-
painted silk flowers are
girly delicious.

HORIZON PLAZA

2 Lee Wing St, Ap Lei Chau, Aberdeen
Open Mon–Sun 10am–7pm

Depending on your shopping stamina, a trip here could make or break you. This very Hong Kong place is less a plaza and more a 28-storey industrial building given over to big-space furniture, food and clothing outlets avoiding the crazy rents in regular shopping strips. Clothing outlets include **Lane Crawford**, **Joyce** (selling Comme des Garçons, Anna Sui and Issey Miyake), **Max Mara**, **Bluebell** (Paul Smith, Jimmy Choo, Moschino), **Diesel** and **Juicy Couture**. Most items are outsized or off-season, so be prepared to hunt. For furniture (that ships) see **Artura Ficus**, which sells bespoke reproduction Chinese wares. **G.O.D.** (*see also* p. 176) has couches and sideboards that blend East and West styles. Pick up a store directory on the ground floor and – given the elevators are tediously slow – work from Tree (*see* p. 167) on the top floor down. Weirdness factor: 11/10.

3.

CASA CAPRIZ

Level 16, Shui Ki Industrial
Building, 18 Wong Chuk
Hang Rd, Aberdeen
9318 1730
www.casacapriz.com
Open Tues–Sat 12–7pm

- -

Designer Irene Capriz (*see*
p. 172) is the visionary
splendid behind this shared
warehouse space devoted to
vintage icons with a strong
design aesthetic. Between
lunch at the Butchers Club
Deli (*see* p. 170) and a feast of
fashion at Ed1tus (*see* p. 164),
tiptoe reverently around 1950s
one-off armchairs and sofas,
wooden dressers and ornate
side tables sourced from
around the globe. Collectibles
abound, including gorgeous
Chinese medicine jars with
metal lids, pendant light
fittings, metal lampshades,
books, typewriters, colonial
fans, retro radios, mirrors and,
my favourite, a 1970s French
ice bucket in the shape of a
pineapple. Everyman pieces
with unpretentious pricing
include sparkling glass orange
squeezers and Italian stovetop
espresso pots.

4.

ED1TUS

Level 16, Shui Ki Industrial
Building, 18 Wong Chuk
Hang Rd, Aberdeen
9760 0437
www.facebook.com/ed1tus
Open Mon–Sun 12–7pm

Evidence that Hong Kong's
global creative community is
fast becoming established can
be found in this 7000-square-
foot multifaceted space.
Ed1tus completes the creative
triumvirate that includes
the Butchers Club Deli (*see*
p. 170) and Casa Capriz (*see*
p. 162). Between them you
can deck out a house, dress
like style snuck up and bit
you on the shoulder pad and
eat well while you're doing
it. Ed1tus appeals to the
modern (gentle) man with
a dozen or so fashion, home
and accessories brands that
scream 'lifestyle'. Pick up a
camel jacket or pinstripe suit
by Mauro Grifoni, a candle
in a handblown glass by Cire
Trudon, a Lumio lampshade
(the kind that folds out
like a fan) or cycling gear
by Martone.

HOT TIP
Aberdeen's Ocean Park attracts more local attention than Hong Kong's Disneyland, perhaps because it's easier to get to. The multistorey aquarium is excellent, as are the rollercoaster and cable car.

5.

MIRTH
Mezzanine, 23 Wong Chuk
Hang Rd, Wong Chuk Hang,
Aberdeen
2553 9811
www.mirthhome.com
Open Mon–Sun 10am–6pm

A surplus of warehouses
and factories has been the
source of (otherwise bland)
Aberdeen's recent creative
impulses. Mirth was the
first to see the potential in
the wide open shop spaces
hidden among dozens of
characterless 1960s buildings.
Formerly a stool factory, this
magical shop with more than
a hint of whimsy has a lovely
girlishness about it – not
necessarily pink, just feminine
with a nod to all ages. It sells
all sorts, from wooden kitchen
tables and coloured metal
chairs to Liberty children's
clothing, colourful pens and
pencils, material-covered
stools, ceramics, wooden toys
and finger puppets. There's a
selection of one-off women's
clothes, plus pretty brooches
and earrings to match.

TREE

Level 28, Horizon Plaza,
2 Lee Wing St, Ap Lei Chau,
Aberdeen
2870 1582
www.tree.com.hk
Open Mon–Sun 10.30am–7pm

New furniture crafted from recycled wood? Who would have thunk it. But call something eco-chic and people start taking an interest. Sitting loftily on the top floor of Horizon Plaza (*see* p. 161), this massive space is expertly curated – more an interior-design store than an obscure warehouse in an industrial zone. Originally selling flawlessly crafted, clean-lined, contemporary furniture, Tree has evolved into an all-things-for-all-homes hub. Shipping is a no-brainer for big items, and there's plenty of small too. Contemporary blue-and-green ginger jars with gold lids, oriental cushions, a tea set sporting the iconic star ferry and a rug featuring the Hong Kong skyline. There are baskets, breadboards and blankets to boot. The spacious kid-friendly coffee shop does coffee, toasties and pastries.

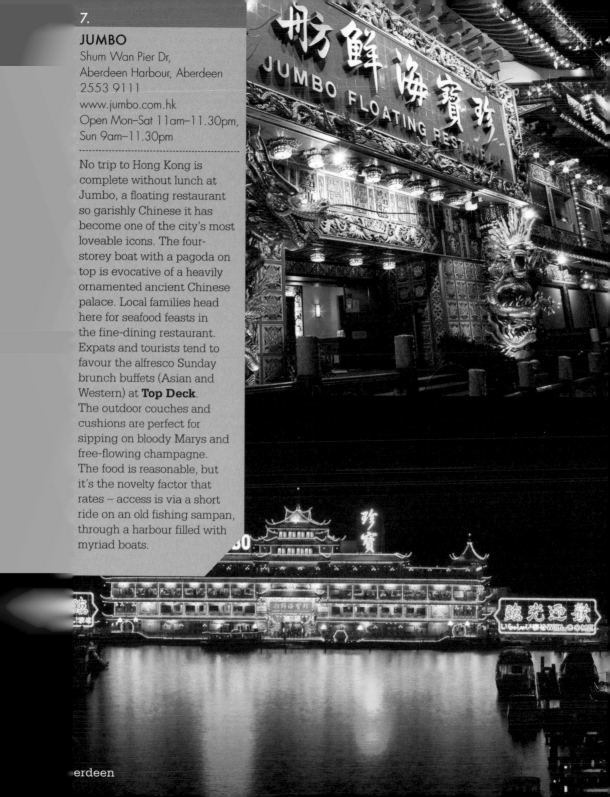

JUMBO

Shum Wan Pier Dr,
Aberdeen Harbour, Aberdeen
2553 9111
www.jumbo.com.hk
Open Mon–Sat 11am–11.30pm,
Sun 9am–11.30pm

No trip to Hong Kong is complete without lunch at Jumbo, a floating restaurant so garishly Chinese it has become one of the city's most loveable icons. The four-storey boat with a pagoda on top is evocative of a heavily ornamented ancient Chinese palace. Local families head here for seafood feasts in the fine-dining restaurant. Expats and tourists tend to favour the alfresco Sunday brunch buffets (Asian and Western) at **Top Deck**. The outdoor couches and cushions are perfect for sipping on bloody Marys and free-flowing champagne. The food is reasonable, but it's the novelty factor that rates – access is via a short ride on an old fishing sampan, through a harbour filled with myriad boats.

8.

THE BUTCHERS CLUB DELI

Level 16, Shui Ki Industrial
Building, 18 Wong Chuk
Hang Rd, Aberdeen
2884 0768
www.butchersclub.com.hk
Open Mon–Sat 11am–4pm

No-one in their right mind
would expect to find the
Butchers Club Deli, located as
it is in a stinker of a high-rise
in the heart of Aberdeen's
bust-your-balls industrial
centre. Thank me later for
sending you there. This New
York–style deli is so cool it
brings a tear to your eye.
Step out of the dodgy lift and
you enter a brave new world
where pollution and traffic
give way to, well, corned beef
and pastrami sandwiches,
dry-aged angus burgers,
charcuterie platters and one
of the best caesar salads
I've ever had the pleasure of
ingesting. Two long tables are
all about sharing your salt and
pepper, and the service is à
la casual – order and pay at
the bar. While you're waiting
for your meal, pop into Casa
Capriz (*see* p. 162) and Ed1tus
(*see* p. 164), partners in cool.

Irene Capriz, from Italy, has always worked in the furniture and design industry. Following a stint in China, she moved to Hong Kong five years ago and, after recognising the lack of quality vintage and design furniture there, opened Casa Capriz (*see* p. 162).

How do you define Hong Kong's style?

It is currently blossoming with independent designers and creative people after being dominated by big names and corporations. At the moment there is a very strong New York influence, especially when it comes to food and beverage. Even so, Hong Kong still manages to keep a strong East-meets-West identity. It is one of the very few cities in Asia where the foreign community is not only transient but has become an integral part of society.

Who are your favourite local designers?

Moustache (*see* p. 038) for its impeccable tailored suits with a vintage twist. I also love the fashion label Tangram, which is

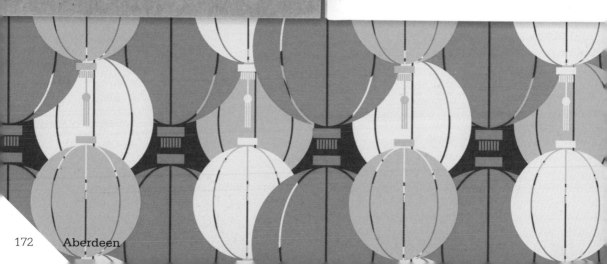

guided by a Colombian duo who fantastically mix their colourful South American heritage with influences from their adopted home town. Sin Sin is a sensational designer with a boutique and an art gallery in Sheung Wan (*see* map on p. 127). It is impossible to leave her shop without falling in love with at least half of it.

What are your favourite Hong Kong places?

The fruit and vegetable market in the neighbourhood of Yau Ma Tei in Kowloon is definitely one of my favourite spots. By 10am all the goods are gone, but you can still see people hanging around for a game of mahjong. I always stop at nearby Mido Cafe (*see* map on p. 203) for a cup of milk tea – it's like being in a Wong Kar-wai (a Hong Kong filmmaker) movie.

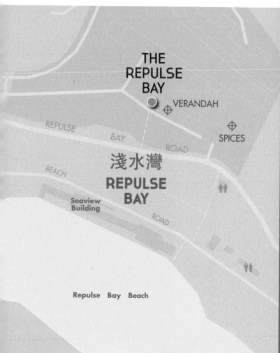

THE
REPULSE
BAY

VERANDAH

REPULSE

BAY

ROAD

SPICES

淺水灣
REPULSE
BAY

BEACH

Seaview
Building

ROAD

Repulse Bay Beach

REPULSE BAY

Known as Chek Chue in Cantonese, Stanley is a well-liked weekend destination on Hong Kong Island. While Stanley Market (see p. 176) attracts tourists looking for cheap clothes, bags and souvenirs, locals flock to the promenade and adjoining piazza. The outdoor restaurants here have views to Blake Pier and Murray House (see p. 180), an imposing colonial building.

Around a couple of stomach-churning bends in the road, Repulse Bay is one of the city's most expensive residential areas and somewhat of a beach resort. For upper-class dining and shops, head to the Repulse Bay (see p. 180). This hard-to-miss building has a large, angular, feng shui hole in it.

STANLEY AND
REPULSE BAY

24   JUN 80T6

SHOP
1 STANLEY MARKET
2 G.O.D.
3 MAMA KID

SHOP, EAT AND DRINK
4 THE REPULSE BAY

17

EAT AND DRINK
5 MURRAY HOUSE
6 THE BOATHOUSE

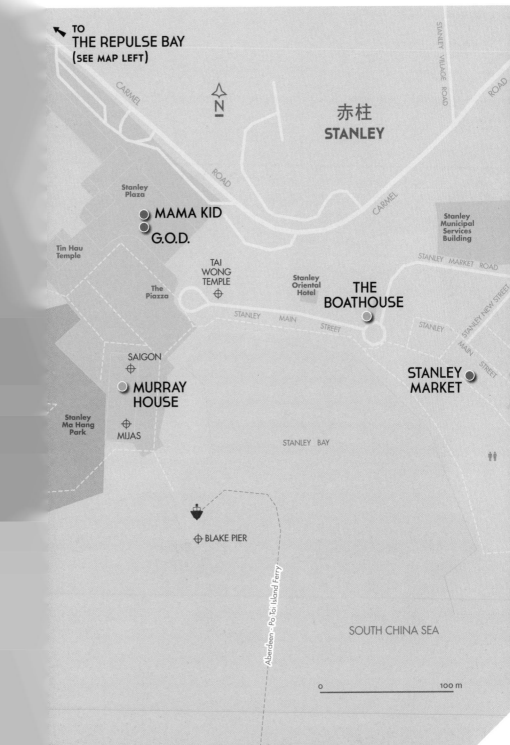

TO
THE REPULSE BAY
(SEE MAP LEFT)

CARMEL

ROAD

STANLEY VILLAGE ROAD

ROAD

N

赤柱
STANLEY

Stanley
Plaza

MAMA KID

G.O.D.

CARMEL

Stanley
Municipal
Services
Building

Tin Hau
Temple

The
Piazza

TAI
WONG
TEMPLE

Stanley
Oriental
Hotel

**THE
BOATHOUSE**

STANLEY MARKET ROAD

STANLEY NEW STREET

STANLEY MAIN STREET

STANLEY

STANLEY

MAIN

STREET

SAIGON

**MURRAY
HOUSE**

**STANLEY
MARKET**

Stanley
Ma Hang
Park

MIJAS

STANLEY BAY

BLAKE PIER

Aberdeen - Po Toi Island Ferry

SOUTH CHINA SEA

0   100 m

1.

STANLEY MARKET
Stanley Main St, Stanley
www.hk-stanley-market.com
Open Mon–Sun 10am–6.30pm

In the mood for hustle, hawking and hyperactivity? This little street market is aimed at tourists, but that doesn't cheapen the experience. Sheltered by old awnings and faded umbrellas, it starts at the roundabout in Stanley Main Street and spreads along the waterfront. The 100-or-so stalls are jam-packed full of hats, bags, clothing, underwear and watches of varying quality. Popular items include imitation Gap children's clothes, Apple accessories, quality linen and Westerner-sized shoes. Did someone say cheap souvenirs? You'll find traditional Chinese fans, silk cheongsams, old Buddhas and jade-esque bangles by the thousands. For something different, perhaps opt for some novelty dim-sum fridge magnets or an Obama in a Mao hat T-shirt.

2.

G.O.D.
Shop 105, Level 1,
Stanley Plaza,
22–23 Carmel Rd, Stanley
2673 0071
www.god.com.hk
Open Mon–Fri 10.30am–8pm,
Sat 10.30am–9pm

G.O.D. is a Hong Kong born and bred furniture, homewares and gift shop that has taken the meaning of 'local' to new heights. The name is clever: it's both an acronym for Goods of Desire and a phonetic rendition of Cantonese slang for 'to live better'. With a strong design element, G.O.D. takes traditional Hong Kong objects and icons and lends them to a modern aesthetic: tenement-house bedspreads, double-happiness Chinese-character umbrellas, market lampshade key chains, panda eye masks, Hong Kong taxi magnets, Chinese poster postcards and Mao badge tote bags. It's the perfect place to buy tasteful souvenirs.

3.

MAMA KID

Shop 103A, Stanley Plaza,
22–23 Carmel Rd, Stanley
2331 8792
www.mamakid.com
Open Mon–Sun 10.30am–7pm

In the thick of Stanley Plaza, Mama Kid stands out as a stylish children's shop devoid of the usual plastic-fantastic kiddie tack. On a little rack of hangers you'll find boys' sweaters and shorts by Mini Rodini and Munsterkids, and printed girls' dresses and skirts by Talc and Anne Kurris. Lightweight Native shoes, hard to come by in Hong Kong, come in all colours, sizes and styles, including the cute boat shoes. The books here are exceptional – hardcover tomes you'll keep forever. Toys include quality kingpins Haba marble slides, Janod pull-along xylophones and happy Herschel backpacks. The fit-out is fun, with bright colours and plenty of low-level shelving so young'uns can tell you exactly what they want for Christmas.

4.

THE REPULSE BAY
Repulse Bay Rd, Repulse Bay
www.therepulsebay.com

The original Repulse Bay Hotel, which stood here from 1920 to 1982, was a colonial beauty. In its heyday it boasted guests such as George Bernard Shaw and Noel Coward, and was immortalised in the classic film *Love is a Many-Splendored Thing*. Today the site boasts a towering apartment building, but the original arcade has stood the test of time. Satiate your sweet tooth with afternoon tea and a glass of bubbles at the **Verandah**, a lovely light-filled space with ceiling fans and views through palm fronds. In the evening, **Spices'** umbrella-clad outdoor setting dishes up Asian cuisine. **Saffron Bakery** in the shopping arcade is good for coffee. It sits alongside fashion boutiques **Tiare** and **Seed**, the **Itsie-Bitsie** gift shop and furniture store **Indigo**.

5.

MURRAY HOUSE
Stanley Plaza,
22–23 Carmel Rd, Stanley
www.hk-stanley-market.com/
Murray-House

Murray House is the big gorgeous bit of Victorian-era eye candy that can sometimes make the rest of Hong Kong look too damn new. It was originally built in Central in 1844 as an officer's quarters. To make way for the new Bank of China building, it was moved in 2002, brick by brick, to Stanley, where it now sits, jutting out onto the water like an old dame reminiscing about her long life. There is a handful of restaurants to check out here, all of them a little more formal than their promenade counterparts. Looking over the water, **Mijas** Spanish restaurant has live music most nights. **Saigon** is an elegant Vietnamese restaurant with ceiling fans and shutters like in the days of yore.

4.

4.

6.

THE BOATHOUSE

88 Stanley Main St, Stanley
2813 4467
www.cafedecogroup.com
Open Mon–Fri
11.30am–10.30pm,
Sat 11am–10.30pm,
Sun 10am–10.30pm

Before the boardwalk promenade was constructed, a visit to this part of Stanley felt like an outing to an old east coast fishing village. Today there's more Hong Kong going on, but the lovely old Boathouse, with its sky-blue Martha's Vineyard–style facade, retains the old beachside vibe. Of the many restaurants and pubs overlooking Stanley Bay, the Boathouse is the most suited to a leisurely lunch and bottle of wine with two alfresco eating options, including a sail-shaded rooftop space. Seafood rules the menu with hits such as salmon and crayfish ravioli, seafood chowder, and king prawns with chorizo, white-bean ragout and paprika.

HOT TIP
For fresh bakery sandwiches, pastries and pies, duck downstairs to the Cave at the market end of Stanley Main Street.

Mark Tjhung, from Perth, Australia, moved to Hong Kong in 2008. That same year *Time Out Hong Kong* launched and went on to become the city's most comprehensive lifestyle publication, with the admirable goal of 'getting to the essence of every element of living in Hong Kong'. Its restaurant guide, in particular, has its finger on the pulse.

What are your favourite Hong Kong cheap eats?

My favourites are in Sheung Wan. Dim Sum Square (*see* map on p. 127) is a wonderful, small yum cha specialist that really represents the best of the casual, all-day dim sum trend that has emerged. Another favourite is Tung Po Kitchen in North Point (see map on p. 116). It's a vast, raucous, down-and-dirty Cantonese dining experience, with exceptional food and an entirely unique atmosphere.

What are your favourite Hong Kong drinking venues?

The Globe (*see* p. 048) is the city's best Brit-style pub, specialising in superb gastropub food and a huge, global array of beer. Club 71 in Soho (*see* map on p. 037) is a modest alleyway bar, which always sports a good vibe and cool, creative people. In Central (*see* map on p. 024), Fu Lu

Shou is my favourite new bar, with excellent fusion cocktails and a splendid terrace. Both Club 71 and Fu Lu Shou are on Hollywood Road.

What are your favourite Hong Kong coffee venues?

The Cupping Room, in Sheung Wan (*see* map on p. 127), is a hip little cafe that serves up some of the best coffee around. Cafe Corridor in Causeway Bay (*see* map on p. 098) is another mainstay of the coffee scene.

Where do you escape to when the city gets too much?

My favourite place is Shek O on the south-eastern tip of Hong Kong Island. The setting is beautiful, the beach is one of the best and the walks around the town itself always make you feel like you're visiting an entirely different country.

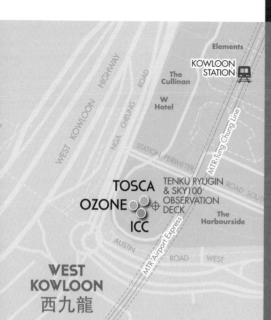

Elements
KOWLOON STATION
The Cullinan
W Hotel
WEST KOWLOON HIGHWAY
NGA CHEUNG ROAD
STATION PERIMETER
MTR-Tung Chung Line
MTR-Airport Express
ROAD SOUTH
TOSCA
OZONE
TENKU RYUGIN & SKY100 OBSERVATION DECK
ICC
The Harbourside
AUSTIN
ROAD WEST

WEST KOWLOON
西九龍

Central might be Hong Kong's top dog but Tsim Sha Tsui, known as TST, is the shih tzu happily yapping at its ankles. Located across Victoria Harbour in the south of Kowloon, TST boasts some of the city's best hotels, while global hot-shot brands like Gucci seem to appear on every corner. The Museum of Art and Cultural Centre are located here, but visitors are more likely to head to the main thoroughfare of Nathan Road to shop and eat.

In West Kowloon, ICC (see p. 189) has given Central's IFC Mall (see p. 012) small-man's syndrome, creating a new home for business, residential, retail and leisure activities.

🚆 TST Station; West Kowloon Station

TSIM SHA TSUI AND WEST KOWLOON

24   JUN 2016

SHOP, EAT AND DRINK
1   1881 HERITAGE & HULLETT HOUSE
2   ICC
3   THE PENINSULA

EAT AND DRINK
4   CUISINE CUISINE
5   DADA BAR & LOUNGE
6   HUTONG
7   LOBBY LOUNGE
8   TOSCA
9   OZONE

17

Kowloon Park Sports Centre & Swimming Pool

Kowloon Park Shopper's Boulevard

OBSERVATORY ROAD

OBSERVATORY ROAD

7-Eleven ■

KIMBERLEY ROAD

Miramar Shopping Centre & Tower

The Luxe Manor

FINDS ⊕

DADA BAR & LOUNGE

KIMBERLEY STREET

KIMBERLEY ROAD

STREET

Kowloon park

CUISINE CUISINE

The Mira

KIMBERLEY STREET

CARNARVON

The One

GRANVILLE ROAD

HAU FOOK STREET

GRANVILLE CIRCUIT

GRANVILLE ROAD

Hong Kong Heritage Discovery Centre

N

NATHAN ROAD

CAMERON LANE

CAMERON ROAD

CAMERON ROAD

AVENUE

TO ICC, OZONE & TOSCA (SEE MAP LEFT)

Kowloon Mosque & Islamic Centre

ⒺⒺ CAMERON

PRAT

HART AVENUE

HAIPHONG ROAD

Ⓔ HUMPHREYS AVENUE

HANOI ROAD

HART AVENUE

SOUTH

CARNARVON ROAD

KOWLOON PARK

ASHLEY ROAD

HANKOW ROAD

LOCK ROAD

Ⓔ

NATHAN ROAD

Ⓔ Ⓔ

The Masterpiece

ⒺⒺ

ROAD

ICHANG STREET

iSQUARE

K11

ⒺⒺ

BRISTOL AVENUE

Ⓔ

The Langham Hong Kong

PEKING ROAD

ROAD

ROAD

Ⓔ Ⓔ MODY

MINDEN AVENUE

MINDEN ROW

CHATHAM ROAD

尖沙咀
TSIM SHA TSUI

HUTONG ○

HANKOW ROAD

ROAD

TSIM SHA TSUI STATION 🚇

Signal Hill Garden

1881 HERITAGE & HULLETT HOUSE ○

MIDDLE ROAD

FELIX & SALON DE NING

7-Eleven ■
MIDDLE ROAD

🚻

EAST TSIM SHA TSUI STATION 🚇

DRIVE

⊕ **THE PENINSULA**

Sheraton Hong Kong Hotel & Towers

MIDDLE ROAD

MTR West Rail Line

ROAD

SALISBURY

Hong Kong Space Museum

Salisbury Garden

0   100 m

CLOCK TOWER ⊕

Hong Kong Cultural Centre

LOBBY LOUNGE ○

Hong Kong Museum of Art

SPOON, NOBU & YAN TOH HEEN ⊕

Intercontinental Hong Kong

Kowloon Public Pier

MTR Tsuen Wan Line

AVENUE OF THE STARS

Tsim Sha Tsui Promenade

1.

1881 HERITAGE & HULLETT HOUSE

2A Canton Rd, Tsim Sha Tsui
2926 8000 (customer service);
3988 0000 (hotel)
www.1881heritage.com;
www.hulletthouse.com
Open Mon–Sun 10am–10pm
(1881 Heritage)

Surrounded by metal-and-glass skyscrapers, neon signs and the toot and hum of TST traffic, this high-end retail and restaurant hub is a slice of tranquillity. Its crowning glory is Hullett House, a luxurious boutique hotel within the old marine police headquarters, a Victorian colonial and neoclassical building that towers over the space. The restaurants found within Hullett House are excellent. The colonial-inspired **Parlour**, with its whirring fans and palms serves high tea along a timeless balcony. **St George** has a degustation menu and **Loong Toh Yuen**, beautifully adorned in traditional Chinese motifs, serves perfect Peking duck. Jewellery and watch brands such as **Tiffany & Co.** and **Cartier** make 1881 a hot spot for Chinese tourists. Expect to see a bride or two in full regalia.

ICC

1 Austin Rd, West Kowloon
2730 0800
www.shkp-icc.com
Open Mon–Sun 24 hrs

Hong Kong's tallest building (at 484 metres or 1587 feet; 118 storeys) looms over West Kowloon and can be seen sparkling and shiny from the far reaches of the city. On floors 102 to 118, the five-star **Ritz-Carlton** hotel is responsible for some of the city's best restaurants (*see* p. 197) and the world's highest bar (*see* p. 198). On the top floor, the **Sky100** observation deck (open 10am to 9pm) has 360-degree bird's-eye views of the city on a clear day. (In lesser weather, visitors will literally be in the clouds, so check the website). Floor 101 is dedicated to dining, with four restaurants including the fabulous Japanese **Tenku RyuGin**. The Kowloon MTR station complex is at the base of ICC, along with **Elements** mall, which has 40 restaurants, 150 retail outlets, an ice-skating rink and the **W Hotel**.

3.

THE PENINSULA
Salisbury Rd, Tsim Sha Tsui
2920 2888
www.peninsula.com

Colonial decadence doesn't get better than the 1928 Peninsula hotel. Stepping into the foyer, with its extravagant staircase, gilt ceilings and string quartet, is to step into history. Most visitors to Hong Kong will find their way here, be it for the eateries, great bars or exclusive shopping arcade (with brands including Baccarat cookware, Taiwanese fashion label Shiatzy Chen, Qeelin and Piaget jewellery and watches, and Michael Kors fashion). The picks include a lavish high tea served with due aplomb by gloved staff in the **Lobby**. Upstairs, **Felix**, a sleek little bar with eye-ogling city views, is sundowner heaven. In the basement, **Salon de Ning** – where 1930s Shanghai glamour meets European ski chalet – has all the ingredients for a red-wine-fuelled night out.

4.

CUISINE CUISINE

The Mira Hotel,
118 Nathan Rd, Tsim Sha Tsui
2315 5222
www.themirahotel.com
Open Mon–Sat
11.30am–2.30pm &
6–10.30pm, Sun
10.30am–3pm & 6–10.30pm

Plush carpets and lounge chairs, glitzy chandeliers, white tablecloths and shimmering glassware – this Cantonese restaurant is a favourite of well-to-do Hong Kong families. Its high-end approach translates to the weekend dim sum, a VIP experience no less. The epicurean dim-sum ingredients are adorned with flower petals and micro herbs and presented as edible works of art that are as easy on the eye as they are on the palate. Lobster and scallop dumplings with truffle and caviar arrive in their own mini steamer; the mustard in the mustard-shrimp dumplings comes in its own tiny dumpling wrapper; and the shrimp dumplings are topped with gold leaf. Dining here really is your good fortune.

5.

DADA BAR & LOUNGE

Level 2, The Luxe Manor,
39 Kimberley Rd, Tsim Sha Tsui
3763 8778
www.dadalounge.com.hk
Open Sun–Thurs 2.30pm–1am,
Fri–Sat 2.30pm–2am

Expect the unexpected. Inspired by the 20th-century dadaist movement, which favoured irrationality over reason, this bar – part of the equally surreal Luxe Manor hotel – is an extravagance, a dark cavernous dreamlike space, the mood of which is wonderfully complemented by stiff drinks. Heart-shaped chairs sprout golden wings, chandelier 'branches' fall from the ceiling, paisley swirls cover the carpet and red-velvet drapes and studded leather panels line the walls. For a bizarre beverage, try the four-man absinthe fountain, which splashes onto spirals of cucumber. Jazz, soul, swing, a cappella and classic-rock artists grace the stage on Fridays and Saturdays. The hotel's Scando restaurant **Finds** is also a good, erm, find.

6.

HUTONG

Level 28, 1 Peking Rd,
Tsim Sha Tsui
3428 8342
www.aqua.com.hk
Open Mon–Sun 12–3pm &
6pm–late

Exit the lift on the 28th floor and, lo and behold, ancient China reveals itself. Sound tacky? It's not. Hutong is one of the city's must-do restaurants because the decadent interior – silk curtains, bamboo birdcages, wood-carved architraves and antique doors – more than lives up to the traditional northern Chinese cuisine. Signature dishes include crispy de-boned lamb (think cold climes) and soft-shell crab served in a basket brimming with red chilli. Wines by the glass include reasonably priced New World and European varieties. Hutong also has some spectacular city-light scenery. Time your run for the neon strobe-light show over Victoria Harbour at 8pm. Failing that, the nightly noodle-pulling display is cheesy but impressive.

7.

LOBBY LOUNGE

Intercontinental, 18 Salisbury Rd, Tsim Sha Tsui

2721 1211

www.hongkong-ic.intercontinental.com

Open Mon–Sun 7am–12.30am

Fact: cocktails taste best when sipped in front of a city skyline. Add a jazz band, tapas canapés and the hum of a contented crowd and you've struck aperitivo gold. This is one of the city's most respectable bars, attracting Intercontinental hotel guests, pre-show diners and those having a drink before dinner at the hotel's Michelin-starred restaurants, **Spoon**, **Nobu** and **Yan Toh Heen**. Its success might be due to it having views minus the vertigo. Sitting on stilts over the water, the floor-to-ceiling windows take in Victoria Harbour's fishing boats and cruise ships, and the neon-striped skyline beyond. It's a mainly seated crowd (on lovely Art Deco lounges), and cocktails have a local touch – try a Fragrant Harbour, Avenue of Stars or Nine Dragons.

TOSCA

Level 102, The Ritz-Carlton,
ICC, 1 Austin Rd, West Kowloon
2263 2270
www.ritzcarlton.com
Open Mon–Sat 12–2.30pm &
6–10.30pm, Sun 11am–3pm
(brunch) & 6–10.30pm

Tosca's petits fours are presented on a fluffy white ball of fairy floss, a cheeky wink to this Italian restaurant's lofty position in the clouds. This is special-occasion territory, heightened by immaculate waiting staff, articulate sommeliers and an abundance of sparkle and glam. The cuisine is Italian with a twist: think antipasto in the form of beef carpaccio with ricotta, spring sprouts, rice crackers and homemade tomato jam. Or savoury tiramisu – a cereal-bar crumble on layers of red-prawn carpaccio, roasted sea scallops, caviar and parsley pasta. The wine list reads like a lesson in Italian regional vineyards. Set menus feature seasonal 'hero' ingredients such as truffle and porcini mushrooms.

OZONE

Level 118, The Ritz-Carlton, ICC,
1 Austin Rd, West Kowloon
2263 2270
www.ritzcarlton.com
Open Mon–Wed 5pm–1am,
Thurs 5pm–2am, Fri 5pm–3am,
Sat 3pm–3am, Sun 12pm–12am

There is no better place to get high, quite literally. Ozone occupies the very top floor of the ICC's (*see* p. 189) Ritz-Carlton at a lofty 484 metres. By rights, it can be called the highest bar in the world, which equates to absolutely spectacular views. The interior is ultra contemporary in a surreal Philippe-Starck-on-acid-in-a-spaceship kind of way, with severe angular lines, a marble bar, abstract neon lighting and metallic cubist furniture. Nab a couch for a laid-back night of cocktails and Japanese titbits. The tuna terrine sashimi goes down well with a vodka Dragontini (with raspberry liqueur, fresh raspberries, a hint of citrus and basil foam).

HOT TIP
Star ferries are famously cheap and endearingly colonial. Grab one between TST and Central for a city view par excellence. Time your run for 8pm and you'll catch the nightly (and slightly gaudy, in a loveable way) laser-and-light show over the harbour.

MEET THE HONGKONGER
TERESA MOON
MIXOLOGIST

Teresa Moon was born in Korea but grew up in Spain's Canary Islands. This cross-cultural exposure ignited a culinary career, which soon morphed into mixology and the art of cocktails. She came to Hong Kong from Barcelona in 2013 and was named one of the city's top 25 bartenders shortly after. She is one of the few female mixologists in Hong Kong and works at Ozone (*see* p. 198).

What's your ideal night out?

I like to try out a couple of new bars in Central with friends: Envoy and Alchemy both offer amazing cocktails with a touch of magic. We usually grab some food as we go. I love Iberico in Soho (*see* map on p. 037) for very well executed Spanish tapas and a comfortable atmosphere. We usually end up at Le Boudoir on Wyndham Street (*see* p. 032), a little bar with a big personality.

What are your favourite Hong Kong eating venues?

Tuk Tuk in Soho, for authentic, homemade Thai food. It reminds me of amazing holidays on Koh Samui! Also Catalunya in Wan Chai for the best Spanish food (when I feel a little homesick).

Where do you escape to when the city gets too much?

I love spending a day on a junk boat with friends and other bartenders. We enjoy sailing away from the city for a few hours, admiring the sea and the weather, and swimming like fish, while invariably mixing drinks on board for each other!

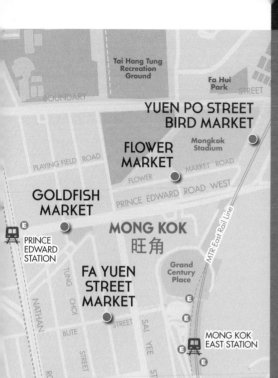

Beyond harbourside Tsim Sha Tsui in Kowloon lie the urban enclaves of Jordan, Yau Ma Tei and Mong Kok, in that order. These heavily populated, traffic-dense neighbourhoods are attractions in their own right, given how different they are from relatively orderly Hong Kong Island. They extend along Nathan Road, so can be explored on foot, but the easiest access points are at eponymous MTR stops on the Tsuen Wan Line.

Outdoor markets are the biggest crowd-pullers. Head to Jordan for the Jade Market (*see p. 205*), Yau Ma Tei for Shanghai Street (*see p. 204*) and Temple Street Night Market (*see p. 210*), and Mong Kok for goldfish, flowers and ladies' goods (*see p. 205*).

Jordan Station;
Yau Ma Tei Station;
Mong Kok Station

JORDAN, YAU MA TEI AND MONG KOK

24   JUN 8ST6

SHOP
1 Shanghai Street
2 Kowloon Street Markets
3 Yue Hwa

SHOP AND EAT
4 Kubrick Café

17

SHOP, EAT AND DRINK
5 Langham Place
6 Temple Street Night Market

EAT AND DRINK
7 Mak Man Kee Noodle Shop

1.

SHANGHAI STREET
Yau Ma Tei
Open Mon–Sun 10am–late

Running parallel to Nathan Road and Temple Street through Jordan, Yau Ma Tei and Mong Kok, Shanghai Street has oodles of history including a row of old tong lau (tenement) shophouses (at numbers 600–626, towards the Mong Kok end). The Yau Ma Tei section is the most popular, it being *the* destination for buying practical kitchenware at wholesale prices. For visitors it's an Aladdin's cave of cheap souvenirs. Trawl both sides of the street for oversized bamboo dim sum steaming baskets, hand-carved wooden mooncake moulds, thick wooden chopping boards and lethal-looking choppers. My personal favourite find is a set of lightweight aluminium beer mugs.

2

KOWLOON STREET MARKETS
Mong Kok and Jordan

To Mong Kok, to Mong Kok, to buy a fat pig. Perhaps not a fat pig but it's certainly possible to pick up a Nemo at the **Goldfish Market**, a finch in a cage at **Yuen Po Street Bird Market** or an auspicious blossom at the **Flower Market**. For something a little more conducive to customs officials, the **Fa Yuen Street Market** has bargain clothing, while the **Ladies Market** is the spot for accessories and beauty products. These markets are all in Mong Kok near the MTR, and are easily explored on foot. The popular **Jade Market** is in Jordan. It's an indoor jewellery market with stalls dripping with colourful beads, big and small. Irene at stall 278 is it-and-a-bit for pearls – you buy 'em, she'll string 'em. Bargaining is essential.

3.

YUE HWA

301–309 Nathan Rd, Jordan
3511 2222
www.yuehwa.com
Open Mon–Sun 10am–10pm

Promised people presents? Yue Hwa is like a Chinese Myer or Marks & Spencer – but with Chinese chintz. This multistorey department store is the place for picking up well-priced gifts and souvenirs, and for finding Chinese products without being bamboozled by bargaining and authenticity. The ground floor has traditional silk dresses, shirts and dressing gowns, and a selection of Chinese medicine, including shark fin, dried abalone and bird's nests (although it's doubtful you'd get such items through customs). Upstairs, the range includes jade and amber bangles, Buddha statues, ornamental sculptures, carved wooden screens, antique pots, kitchen ceramics, tea sets, fans and chopsticks. Pajamas and silk quilts are here too. Oh, and mahjong sets and antique snuff bottles and …

4.

KUBRICK CAFÉ

Prosperous Garden,
3 Public Square St, Yau Ma Tei
2384 8929
www.kubrick.com.hk
Open Mon–Sun
11.30am–10pm

Broadway Cinematheque (www.cinema.com.hk) is Hong Kong's last remaining alternative cinema with four screens showing a line-up of quality mainstream and arthouse flicks, classic films and film-festival favourites. Fittingly, this cultural hub, located unassumingly in the middle of estate housing, is also home to fabulous Kubrick Café, where arty types, cinephiles and students sip matcha (green-tea) frappé coffee and ice tea (or eat pastries and toasted sandwiches). The cafe is huge and filled with books devoted to (mostly Western) films and their directors, like Coppola, Tarantino, Hitchcock and Bergman. There is also a pop-up shop (sustainable beauty products and produce on my last visit) and a comprehensive DVD selection.

3.

4.

HOT TIP
For a Hong Kong cooking course, go no further than Martha Sherpa (www. marthasherpa.com). She has a kitchen in the heart of Mong Kok where she teaches traditional Chinese cooking techniques with an iron fist.

5.

LANGHAM PLACE

555 Shanghai St, Mong Kok
3552 3388
www.langhamhotels.com
Open Mon–Sun
11am–11pm (mall)

In one of the busiest urban environments in the world, sparklingly modern Langham Place is somewhat of a landmark. The 15-storey mall has a futuristic central escalator delivering shoppers to sportswear, lingerie, handbag, shoe, beauty and electronic stores and outlets. Accessible via a glass walkway, the adjoining Langham Place Hotel takes its locale seriously with its extensive collection of Chinese art including works by Jiang Shuo and Yue Minjun. **Ming Court** is its lauded Cantonese restaurant with specialities like giant garoupa fish enrobed in minced shrimp, and coral trout fillet with Chinese black mushroom and dried shrimp roe. Ming Court's cellar has a bottle of Petrus Pomerol from Bordeaux, a HK$43,000 tipple.

6.

TEMPLE STREET NIGHT MARKET

Temple Street, Yau Ma Tai
Open Mon–Sun 6–10pm

- -

Dai pai dongs or street food markets used to be popular at the end of a working day, but then the Hong Kong government decided to clean up the streets. Mercifully this market remains. Stretching from Man Ming Lane South to Nanking Street (with a temple in the middle), this outdoor eatery takes over the neighbourhood at sundown. Order takeaway oyster pancakes and won tons, or sit down at formica tables for a causal banquet of whole steamed fish, clams sautéed in garlic, and fried rice. Tsingtao longneck beers are the beverage of choice. After dinner, stroll around the canvas-topped stalls selling everything from souvenirs, cheap handbags and clothing to gadgets and electronics.

MAK MAN KEE NOODLE SHOP

51 Parkes St, Jordan
2736 5561
Open Mon–Sun 12pm–12.30am

It's essential to know the closest good won-ton noodle shop no mater which corner of Hong Kong you find yourself in. Mak Man Kee is spot-on for local ambience, its narrow space lit by fluoro lighting and crowded with booths, and its teeny steamy kitchen tucked behind glass as you walk in. It's all very Hong Kong retro. Order the won-ton noodle soup; the noodles should be springy and al dente and Mak's don't disappoint. Another telltale thumbs up is the crunch when you bite into the prawn won ton. Also, note the delicately thin wrappers. The portions are small, so top up with a side of greens. Break out some mangled Cantonese and you'll get smiles from the staff.

The fact that Ken Suen was born and bred in Hong Kong, and educated in the US, is highlighted in his personal style, a co-mingling of old Hong Kong layered with American fashion and culture. It's this combination that became the inspiration for his shop WDSG (*see* p. 072).

How do you define Hong Kong's style?

Hong Kong is truly metropolitan; you can find a lot of different cultures and styles in a small place. But people here are also big-time trend followers, from the Japanese-style trend ten years ago, when the brand I.T. (*see* p. 102) became popular, to the foreign-designer-brands trend, then to fast fashion like Zara and H&M in Central. Now, it's Korean K-pop … people adapt and forget and this cycle just goes on and on …

What are your favourite Hong Kong shopping venues?

I personally like small shops and finding unknown and undiscovered brands. I like going to Star Street in Wan Chai (*see* map on p. 065), and, in Sheung Wan, Gough Street (*see* p. 134). Sometimes I also go to very local places like Sham Shui Po, which is two stops from Mong Kok on the MTR. You might be surprised at the fabrics and items you can find there.

Who are your favourite designers?

I prefer foreign brands. I am a fan of Ralph Lauren and Paul Smith, and lately I also like Jason Denham.

澳門
MACAU

RUINS OF
ST. PAUL'S

MERCEARIA PORTUGUESA

MACAUSOUL

MOUNT
FORTRESS

ALBERGUE 1601

RUA DA FELICIDADE

AVENIDA DE ALMEIDA

7-Eleven

SERGIO

ST. JOSEPH'S
SEMINARY
& CHURCH

7-Eleven

STANLEY HO

ST. LAWRENCE'S
CHURCH

HARBOUR

Luis
De Camoes
Garden

ESTRADA DO REPOUSO

RUA DO CAMPO

RIBEIRO

INNER

ALMIRANTE

RUA DO

AVENIDA DOUTOR

285 SIGNUM LIVING STORE

A-MA
TEMPLE

Sai
Van
Lake

Nam
Van
Lake

MACAU

Sixty kilometres (37 miles) south-west of Hong Kong, Macau consists of a peninsula that narrowly borders China's Guangdong province, and the islands of Taipa and Coloane, which have been connected by a section of casino-studded landfill known as the Cotai strip.

Much is said about Macau's gambling dens, the most elaborate of which, the Venetian, is bigger than its Las Vegas counterpart. But the real drawcard to this former Portuguese colony and China's only other Special Administrative Region is its seamless blend of Portuguese and Cantonese influences. An overnight trip here can reveal a tantalising combination of East meets West in the architecture, the cuisine, and the people and their unique culture.

24   JUN 8076

SHOP
1 285 Signum Living Store
2 Cunha Bazaar
3 Mercearia Portuguesa
SHOP AND EAT
4 Rua da Felicidade

17

EAT
5 Lord Stow's Bakery
EAT AND DRINK
6 António
7 Restaurante Fernando
8 Albergue 1601

CUNHA
BAZAAR

氹仔
TAIPA

Taipa
Grande

Macau
International
Airport

Macau
Jockey
Club

Macau
Stadium

ANTÓNIO

Macau
University of
Science and
Technology

TO
MERCEARIA
PORTUGUESA,
ALBERGUE 1601,
RUA DA FELICIDADE,
& 285 SIGNUM
LIVING STORE
(SEE MAP LEFT)

Galaxy
Macau

TASTING
ROOM

City of
Dreams

The
Venetian
Macau

Four
Seasons
Hotel
Macau

Sands
Cotai
Central

AVENIDA CIDADE NOVA

AVENIDA

AVENIDA DE
COTAI

路氹城
COTAI

ESTRADA DO ISTMO

AVENIDA DO PROGRESSO

AVENIDA DA NAVE DESPORTIVA

RUA DO TIRO

RUA DA PATINAGEM

Macau
East
Asian
Games
Dome

PONTE
FLOR DE LOTUS

AVENIDA MARGINAL

FLOR

DE

LOTUS

ESTRADA   FLOR   DE   LOTUS

Ka Ho
Reservoir

N

Caesars
Golf
Macau

Coloane
Karting
Track

Seac Pai Van
Reservoir

ESTRADA DO ISTMO

ESTRADA   DO   ALTINHO   DE   KA   HO

HENGQIN
UNDERWATER
TUNNEL

RUA MARGINAL DA CONCORDIA

ESTRADA DE SEAC PAI VAN

ESTRADA ALTO

Seac
Pai
Van Park

GIANT PANDA
PAVILION

A-MA
STATUE

Hac Sa
Reservoir

HAC SA

Macau
Tin Hau
Temple

Alto De
Coloane

Hac Sa
Beach

LORD
STOW'S
BAKERY

COLOANE
TRAIL

ESTRADA DE COLOANE

路環
COLOANE

ESTRADA DE CHEOC VAN

RESTAURANTE
FERNANDO

ESTRADA DE HAC SA

HAC SA BAY

0   500 m

1.

285 SIGNUM LIVING STORE

285 Rua do Almirante Sérgio,
Macau City Centre
(853) 2896 8925
www.signum.mo
Open Mon–Sun 12–8pm

Standing in a row of crusty
old shophouses complete
with lanterns, window cages,
exposed air-conditioner units
and plantation shutters, this
homewares-y, artsy, design-y
shop is a surprisingly modish
find. Tabletops and shelves
are lovingly stocked with
creative intrigues such as
enamel cups and plates
with abstract animal prints,
glass bottles that look like
the plastic variety, and old
tea cups and saucers sliced
in half then re-partnered
with mismatched results.
It's not all whimsical though.
Metallic pendant lights would
make great gifts, as would
the stationery and envelope
openers, bold cushions and
wooden toys for kids. Signum
is big on promoting local
artists whose work lines
the walls.

2.

CUNHA BAZAAR

33–35 Rua do Cunha, Taipa
(853) 2882 7989
www.cunhabazaar.com
Open Mon–Sun 9.30am–10pm

Painted bright yellow and
covered in murals, two-
storey Cunha Bazaar has
become a landmark in old
Taipa, specialising in made-
in-Macau merchandise.
Downstairs, polished-
concrete floors and nostalgic
wallpaper provide the
setting for Macau's offbeat
culinary treats – spicy
dried fish, shrimp-flavoured
peanuts and coconut egg
rolls with shredded pork
jerky, all packaged to take
home. Upstairs a slightly
kitsch space is dedicated to
Macau's iconic Soda Panda
TV cartoon characters, with
gimmicky T-shirts, postcards
and almond cakes in retro
boxes. **Rua do Cunha's**
traditional Macau morsels
include almond cookies with
pork filling, ginger candy and
durian agar-agar pudding.

1.

2.

HOT TIP
For refined wines, leather couches, jazz and charcuterie, pop into MacauSoul (31A Rua de Sao Paulo), a music lover's lounge in the city.

CUNHA BAZAAR

3.

MERCEARIA PORTUGUESA

8 Calçada da Igreja de São Lázaro, Macau City Centre
(853) 2856 2708
http://merceariaportuguesa.com
Open Mon–Fri 1–9pm, Sat–Sun 12–9pm

Macau's St Lazarus neighbourhood could well be called Little Lisboa, such is the character and beauty of its 16th-century cobbled streets and shuttered low-rise houses. In the middle of it is Albergue da Santa Casa da Misericórdia, an enchanting Portuguese square shaded by a camphor tree and bordered by a handful of businesses including Albergue 1601 (*see* p. 224) and Mercearia Portuguesa (aka the Portuguese Corner Shop). A visit should induce some serious mother-country nostalgia. On old-school wooden shelves you'll find spicy Portuguese sardines, bottles of olive oil, pickled green tomatoes, decadently wrapped chocolates and old-fashioned bon bons. Goods with a Macau touch include Portuguese tiles, retro hand soaps and handmade toys.

RUA DA FELICIDADE
Macau City Centre

For whatever reason, this little street – one of old Macau's most emblematic – has not made the World Heritage register. It will in time, no doubt. A couple of blocks off Avenida de Almeida Ribeiro and a five-minute walk from famous **Senado Square**, Rua da Felicidade is a thin strip of two-storey, tile-roofed tong lau (Chinese shophouses) with red shutters, doors and awnings. It was once a hangout for prostitutes, opium dealers, drinkers and gamblers, and thus the name translates to 'Happiness Street'. The rejuvenated version is a serene place to amble past fish tanks, noodle restaurants, bubble teashops and bakeries where the homely smell of fresh-baked almond cookies fills the air.

5.

LORD STOW'S BAKERY

1 Rua do Tassara, Coloane
(853) 2888 2534
www.lordstow.com
Open Mon–Sun 7am–10pm

In 1989, English expat Andrew Stow created a hybrid recipe between Portuguese pastel de nata and English custard tarts. To differentiate between the familiar local 'egg tart', resident Chinese people dubbed them 'Portuguese egg tarts'. Stow's recipe caught on in Macau and became an edible icon for visitors and locals alike. The company that produces the tarts, Lord Stow's Bakery, has outlets in Hong Kong, Korea, Japan, Taiwan and the Philippines and sells 10,000 pieces on average each day. This bakery is the original, but there are four other local offshoots, two of which are nearby.

6.
ANTÓNIO

7 Rua dos Clerigos,
Old Taipa Village, Taipa
(853) 2899 9998
www.antoniomacau.com
Open Mon–Sun 12–3pm &
6–10.30pm

Only minutes away from the
Cotai Strip, Old Taipa Village
is an unexpected local gem
with quaint alleys, renovated
Chinese shophouses and
colonial buildings all aglow
with street lamps. Among
the bars and restaurants
is António's, a Portuguese
restaurant with exterior
mosaic tiles and wooden
wine kegs. António Coelho
has won accolades for
his authentic cuisine and
excellent service (he waited
on my table each time I
visited). Signature dishes
include goat's cheese au
gratin with olive oil and
honey on toast for starters,
and charcoal-grilled sardines
with a potato and green-
pepper salad for main. The
wine list has a Euro bent.

7.
RESTAURANTE FERNANDO

9 Praia de Hac Sa, Coloane
(853) 2899 9998
www.fernando-restaurant.com
Open Mon–Sun 12–9.30pm

Hongkongers take daytrips to
Macau just to have lunch at
Fernando's – it's almost a rite
of passage. This is Macau's
most famed restaurant, a
no-fuss, no-reservations
venue that promises a rare
breed of casual dining. Locals
tend to sit up front in a plain
room with yellow bricks and
louvre windows, but the rear
is better. Out back there's
a beer garden and a faux
rustic pavilion with ceiling
fans, dark-wood beams,
high ceilings and chequered
tablecloths. Wherever you sit,
the Portuguese fare stacks
up, be it salty baccalau (cod)
or stuffed octopus stew and a
jug of sangria. Finish with a
walk on the fine black sand of
Hac Sa Beach.

6.

7.

8.

ALBERGUE 1601

8 Calçada da Igreja de São
Lázaro, Macau City Centre
(853) 2836 1601
www.albergue1601.com
Open Tues–Thurs & Sun
12–11pm, Fri–Sat 12–11.30pm

Pull up an alfresco pew at
Albergue 1601 and behold the
European scenery: a mosaic
cobbled square surrounded
by two-storey Portuguese
terraces with buttery yellow
walls and wooden shutters.
This beautiful restaurant
taps into the Zeitgeist of
Macau's Portuguese history
with its Portuguese-skewed
Mediterranean food. Linger
at lunch over caldo verde
(potato and kale soup) and
vieira ao forno (jumbo scallops
with garlic and Portuguese
sausage). In the evenings,
indoor tables are laid with
white linen and shimmering
glassware. It's very romantic.
Pair roasted rack of lamb,
chilli king prawns or grilled
black pork with European
wines from a cellar lining
one wall.

MEET THE HONGKONGER
KONSTANTIN BESSMERTNYI
ARTIST

Russian-born Konstantin Bessmertnyi grew up in Blagoveshchensk, near the China border, and completed his Masters at the Vladivostok Art Academy. After success working as an artist, he came to Macau by invitation from the Macau government in 1992. 'I never imagined I would settle down in a studio in this remote Portuguese colony', he said. But he did.

Why did you settle in Macau?

There was something captivating and mysterious that always kept me in Macau, despite many other opportunities in other places. Today most of my inspiration comes from here. I see this place as a miniature 'sin city' with a very distinct social pyramid that displays all possible human actions in extreme conditions.

What's your take on the city?

The city is rapidly changing into the gambling capital of the world and much of the attention has been focused on improving all the industries that accompany gambling. However, there is a handful of islands that are trying to resist the changes by retaining their culture.

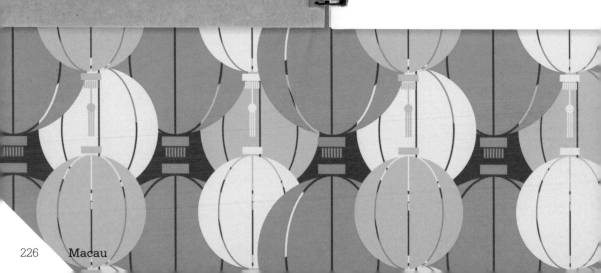

What are your favourite Macau experiences?

I am often in Europe and have eaten many great meals, but one overrides all others: an extravagant meal in the Tasting Room at City of Dreams on the Cotai strip (Avenida de Cotai, *see* map on p. 215). I have favourite hikes too. Visitors should attempt parts of the Coloane Trail, which begins on Estrada do Alto de Coloane and meanders around the island.

GETTING TO AND FROM HONG KONG INTERNATIONAL AIRPORT

Hong Kong International Airport, known as Chek Lap Kok (www.hkairport.com), is located 45 kilometres from central Hong Kong on Lantau Island. It is lauded as one of the world's best airports with efficient baggage reclaim and typically queue-less customs terminals. Following are some options for getting to and from Chep Lap Kok:

Airport Express

Almost always the best option, this train whisks passengers from the airport into Hong Kong MTR station (via Tsing Yi and Kowloon stations) every 10 to 12 minutes between 5.54am and 12.48am Monday to Sunday. The entire journey takes 24 minutes (which is much quicker than a taxi) and costs HK$100 one-way. You can also purchase a tourist pass (see www.mtr.com.hk), which offers return Airport Express tickets and three days of unlimited MTR travel from HK$220.

On leaving, Hong Kong and Kowloon MTR stations have free check-in services open 24 to 1.5 hours before departure. It's spectacularly functional and means you can jump onto the Express to the airport baggage-free.

Taxi

Taxis are very accessible from the airport, and are not overly expensive. Follow the signs to the queue (it's never very long). Red taxis service Hong Kong Island and Kowloon, blue taxis service Lantau Island and green taxis service the New Territories. Fares are metered and getting ripped off is rare. The journey to central Hong Kong will cost between HK$300 and HK$400 including tolls, plus HK$5 extra for each piece of luggage in the boot. The journey time is about 45 minutes; add an extra 30 minutes if you're hitting the city during peak times.

GETTING AROUND TOWN

Diverse yet efficient is the catchcry for Hong Kong transport, a combination of underground railway (MTR), light rail, buses, minibuses, ferries, trams and (the world's longest) escalator. It's worth buying an Octopus card (www.octopuscards.com) for hassle-free access to all modes of transport. A scanner will automatically deduct payments.

MTR

The MTR (www.mtr.com.hk) has nine clean and efficient underground lines (including the East Rail Line for travel between Hong Kong and Shenzhen) and an Airport Express link. It boasts 'passengers consistently arriving at their destinations on time 99% of the time'.

BUSES

Air-conditioned one- and two-deck buses crisscross main streets throughout Hong Kong Island and the New Territories stopping at well-signed dedicated bus stops. Fares are based on distance. Minibuses require a bit more local knowledge. They cater to small streets and can be flagged down. Once they're full, minibuses won't stop for a new passenger until a seat becomes available. Green minibuses have specific routes at fixed prices, whereas red minibus routes are not always fixed and passengers can get on and off anywhere along the route. You pay as you alight on red minibuses and the driver can usually provide change for small notes.

FERRIES

Star Ferries

Star Ferries (www.starferry.com.hk) service Victoria Harbour with piers at Tsim Sha Tsui, Central and Wan Chai. They run between 7.30am and 11.30pm Monday to Friday, depending on the route, with shortened hours on weekends. The double-decker green vessels act mainly as commuter transport but a trip is a must-do for tourists. The fares are famously low.

Outlying Island Services

Ferries operating from the Central ferry piers near IFC Mall on Hong Kong Island provide services to Peng Chau, Cheung Chau, Lamma Island and Lantau Island, including Discovery Bay. Two types of ferries operate along most routes: standard ferries and the slightly more expensive fast ferries. At least one island outing is a Hong Kong must.

Macau Ferries

Two ferry companies service the Hong Kong Island–Macau route. Ferries depart from the Macau Ferry Terminal on Connaught Road in Central every 15 minutes from 7am to 12am. The trip takes approximately one hour. Tickets cost about HK$300 one-way and can be bought from self-service ticket kiosks at the terminal. With a valid ticket, you can take an earlier ferry if there are seats available. Don't forget your passport!

PEAK TRAM

Opened in 1988, the old-school Peak Tram (open 7am to 12am Monday to Sunday) departs every 10 to 15 minutes from the lower Peak Tram terminus on Garden Road, Central. The seven-minute journey through skyscrapers and rainforest is at an almost impossible angle, making this the steepest funicular railway in the world. It's worthwhile doing once, but beware the queues.

MID-LEVELS ESCALATOR

The Mid-Levels escalator is a commuter mover that runs between Queens Road Central and Conduit Road in Mid-Levels, bisecting 14 streets in the process. It operates between 6am and midnight Monday to Sunday (downhill 6am to 10am, uphill 10.30am to 12am). It's an excellent option for tourists exploring the steep streets of Soho.

TRAMS

Trams (www.hktramways.com) traverse east–west across Hong Kong Island on six routes (covering 30 kilometres) that run between Shau Kei Wan, Happy Valley and Kennedy Town. At peak hours you'll be lucky to bag a seat but in down times, a front seat on the top deck is a window into the frenetic and varied street life of Hong Kong. Trams run from 5am to 12am Monday to Sunday, and cost HK$2.30/1.20 (adult/child) per trip. Pay as you get off.

WALKING

You'll do a lot of walking in Hong Kong – it's how you'll stumble across some of your best finds – so wear a good pair of shoes and carry bottled water with you. Avoid jaywalking at major crossings in Central, as fines are readily issued if you're caught.

TAXIS

Taxis are easy to flag down and cheap compared with other large cities. An average ride on Hong Kong Island costs approximately HK$30 to HK$50.

TAXI TIPS

Taxis are usually easily hailed along the street, but taxi queues and taxi stands are common at hotels, train stations and shopping malls.

Taxis are 'available' when the rooftop light is on and a red circular sign in the front window is showing. Rectangular red signs in the front window denote Kowloon taxis. If you catch one of these from Hong Kong Island to Kowloon or vice versa you only pay tunnel tolls for one direction.

If you're on Hong Kong Island and want to go to Kowloon, or vice versa, hail an obliging cab by making a wavy motion with your hand to denote going under the water and through the tunnel. It's local knowledge.

Taxi doors open and close on their own! Ask your hotel clerk or concierge to tell taxi drivers where you are going.

Take your hotel business card with you when going out and give it to taxi drivers when you want to get back to your hotel.

CRIME

Crime is low in Hong Kong. There are very few dangerous areas. And if you leave anything in a taxi, chances are the driver will drop it back to you. Police officers frequently patrol many areas and are both professional and helpful.

ARTS & ABOUT

There is an art scene in Hong Kong and there are plenty of festivals, but they can be hard to pin down. The following should set you in the right direction:

HK (www.hk-magazine.com) An oft-irreverent expat magazine.

South China Morning Post (www.scmp.com) The city's major English-language daily broadsheet.

The List (www.thelist.com.hk) A free mag with definitive lists of Hong Kong's shops and services.

FESTIVALS AND EVENTS

Chinese New Year (late January/early February)

Hong Kong Arts Festival (www.hk.artsfestival.org; February/March)

Hong Kong International Film Festival (www.hkiff.org.hk; March/April)

Cheung Chau Bun Festival (April/May/June)

Hong Kong International Art Fair (www.hongkongartfair.com; May)

Affordable Art Fair Hong Kong (http://affordableartfair.com/hongkong; May)

Dragon Boat Festival (June)

Mid-Autumn Festival (late September/early October)

Star Street Gourmet & Wine Walk (www.starstreet.com.hk; October)

Clockenflap (www.clockenflap.com; October/November) An awesome offbeat music festival.

EATING AND DRINKING

Menus at international restaurants in Hong Kong are written in English and many local venues also have an English-version menu under the counter. In this book, we've broken listings down as follows: places listed under an Eat heading don't sell alcohol, but often serve tea and coffee; those listed under Eat and Drink serve food, tea and coffee (usually), and booze.

HYGIENE

After the SARS epidemic in 2002, Hongkongers became fastidious about hygiene. Public washrooms and hand sanitisers can be found at most tourist sites and in shopping malls. Lift buttons and escalator handrails are all slavishly wiped down regularly.

WATER

Hong Kong tap water conforms to the World Health Organisation's recommended guidelines for drinking-water quality, but it doesn't taste great. Some restaurants and bars will supply tap water on request. When they don't, it's usually because plumbing systems in the older buildings can render the water undrinkable. Bottled water is readily available in restaurants, supermarkets and so on.

EATING AND DRINKING TIPS

Most restaurants, cafes and bars in Hong Kong are open seven days a week (if they shut it will usually be on a Monday or Tuesday). They tend to open late, around 11am and close around 10pm. Unless foreign-operated, cafes don't open until midday or later – locals tend to drink their coffee around 3pm.

In the higher-end restaurants and bars it's almost always a good idea to book ahead, especially on Friday and Saturday nights. There is a new school of hip bars and restaurants that won't take bookings. These should probably be avoided on weekends unless, of course, you're okay with getting sloshed at the bar while you're waiting for a table.

Smoking is not allowed inside restaurants and bars, but many venues have an alfresco area for this purpose.

Chopstick etiquette: when using chopsticks, don't stick them upright in a bowl of rice – this is a funeral custom. Also, don't pass food to or take food from other people using your own chopsticks – look for the communal chopsticks next to each dish (they're usually a different colour).

Pour other people's drinks – especially tea – as much as possible.

At markets and noodle shops you'll sometimes be given a bowl of hot water to wash your own rice bowls and chopsticks. This is customary, a hangover from less hygienic times. Roll with it by giving your utensils a dip, then the water will be taken away.

MANNERS

Manners are important in Hong Kong, so always be as polite as possible, especially to the elderly. 'Face' is everything, so avoid losing your cool at all costs, despite the frustrations a different culture can throw at you.

Take off your shoes before entering a house.

If you're sick with a cold, buy a face mask – they're to protect other people, not you.

While shopping, it is routine for shop assistants to follow you around the store so they're at the ready when you have a question. In some other countries, this might only happen if you're suspected of being a shoplifter. Best to grin and bear it.

PUBLIC HOLIDAYS

Most shops and restaurants remain open during public holidays, though some might close for two days over Chinese New Year. Some traditional shops and restaurants and small family-owned restaurants may stay closed for longer at this time. For a full list of public holidays visit www.gov.hk/en/about/abouthk/holiday.

MONEY

Hong Kong's currency is the Hong Kong dollar. It is pegged to the US dollar at a rate of about HK$7.80 to US$1, although exchange rates fluctuate slightly. It comes in denominations of HK$1000, HK$500, HK$100, HK$50, HK$20 and HK$10 in notes, and HK$10, HK$5, HK$2, HK$1, HK$0.50, HK$0.20 and HK$0.10 in coins.

The currency is used in both Hong Kong and Macau, as the two regions are of close proximity and their currencies have similar exchange rates.

At Hong Kong International Airport, currency exchange counters are open from early morning until late at night and many located within the city stay open into the evening.

Most ATMs take international cards and can be found on streets and outside banks. You'll also find ATMs in 7-Elevens.

Tipping is big in Hong Kong. A 10% tip will be automatically added to your bill, and often people tip another 5% to 10% on top of this. More recent hipster venues are boasting 'no service charges', instead asking customers to judge the service. Unless you have a bad experience, it would be considered pretty tight to not tip.

TELEPHONE

Hong Kong's country code is 852. To call outside Hong Kong dial '+' then the country code or '001' then the country code. All phone numbers, including mobiles, have eight digits. GSM-compatible phones can be used in Hong Kong. The network coverage includes tunnels and the MTR.

SIM cards can be purchased at 7-Eleven or Circle K stores relatively cheaply (approximately HK$100) with minimal administration. Even better, Discover Hong Kong Tourist SIM Cards (www.discoverhongkong.com) offer all-inclusive and immediately accessible five-day (HK$69) and eight-day (HK$118) packages, including a Macau data-roaming package.

Given almost everyone in Hong Kong has a mobile, public phones are fast becoming redundant, however, phone-card and coin-operated phones can still be found at MTR stations and major shopping hubs.

USEFUL PHRASES

Cantonese people rarely expect *gweilos* (foreigners) to speak their lingo as the nine tones make it a difficult language to master. On Hong Kong Island, most people in hotels and the wider service industry will usually speak some English. Taxi drivers will speak just enough to get you to your destination. But like anywhere, it's always appreciated when you have a go, so give some of these basic sayings a try.

Hello: lay ho

How are you?: lay gay ho a maa?

Good morning: jo san

Goodbye: baai baai

Thank you: ng goy

The bill please?: my dun?

Stop here: leedo

Keep the change: mmsay ee jow

How much is it?: gay daw chin?

Where is the ... ?: hai bin doe ...?

Airport: gay cheung

Bus stop: baa si jaam

Post office: yau guk

Hotel: jau dim

Subway station: day tit jaam

ATM: ji dung tai fun gay

TOURIST INFORMATION

Tourist Information Centres are located at Hong Kong International Airport (Transfer Area E2, Buffer Halls A and B, Arrivals Level T1; open 8am to 9pm Monday to Sunday), the Peak Piazza (between the tower and galleria; open 11am to 8pm Monday to Sunday) and Star Ferry Concourse (Tsim Sha Tsui, Kowloon; open 8am to 8pm Monday to Sunday). Leaflets and online information are available 24 hours at these venues. Tours can also be booked at all visitor centres.

Hong Kong visitors can also call the multilingual tourist hotline (2508 1234) between 9am and 6pm Monday to Sunday. The tourism board website (www.discoverhongkong.com) is a decent source of easily navigable information.

WI-FI

Internet access is fast, reliable and often free in Hong Kong. Most hotels and hostels have internet facilities and many coffee shops, cafes and pubs have free wi-fi where courtesy dictates you buy a drink or snack. You can connect to the internet with a mobile device near the 'MTR Free Wi-Fi Hotspot' sign in every MTR station. It offers free connectivity for 15 minutes per session, with a maximum of five sessions per smart phone/iPad/device per day.

ELECTRICAL APPLIANCES

The majority of electrical outlets in Hong Kong take a three-pronged UK-style plug.

GPS

Smart-phone GPS devices are unreliable in Hong Kong, due to the height and density of the city's buildings. Use an old-fashioned map instead.

EMERGENCIES

Call 999 for local police, ambulance service, fire department and other emergency services.

ABOUT THE AUTHOR

Penny Watson

Hong Kong makes fascinating fodder for a freelance journalist and travel writer – during my six years living and working in the city, I was never short on a story. I made dim sum in Kowloon; camped on the remote beaches of Sai Kung; practised tai chi; learned the art of tea ceremonies; ate my weight in street food; interviewed some extraordinary people; and reviewed dozens of restaurants and hotels. The upshot of all this on-the-ground research, is a passion – an infatuation really – for this most brilliant of Asian cities.

While I have a sizeable portfolio of newspaper and magazine articles and a handful of guidebooks under my belt, *Hong Kong Precincts* was my first solo project. It was commissioned shortly before I moved back to my hometown of Melbourne. By the time I had researched, written and signed off on the manuscript I had made that journey home, the bridge between two very different worlds. So this book has become my swan song of sorts, a homage to the wondrous places unearthed during six remarkable years in the city. Its pages are packed full of memories that tap into friendships and faces and unforgettable experiences. I hope some of this ardour for the city rubs off so that you come to know and love Hong Kong too.

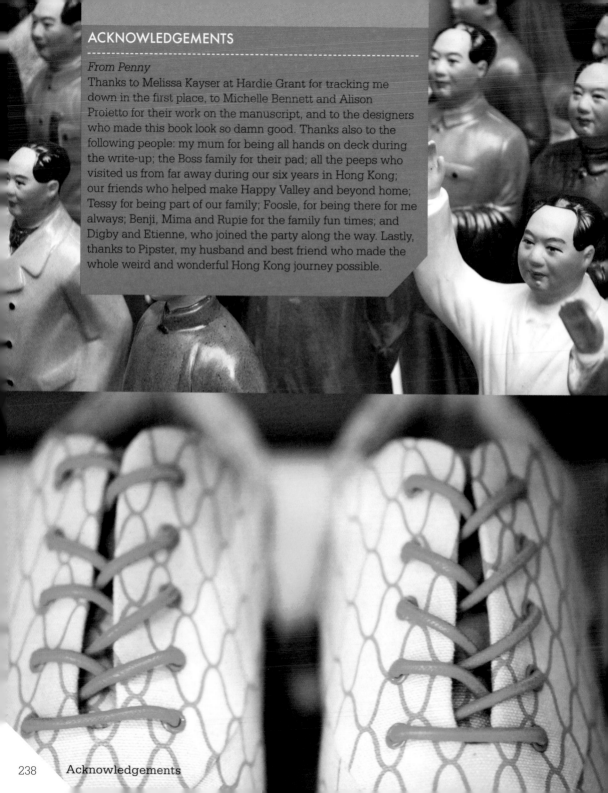

ACKNOWLEDGEMENTS

From Penny

Thanks to Melissa Kayser at Hardie Grant for tracking me down in the first place, to Michelle Bennett and Alison Proietto for their work on the manuscript, and to the designers who made this book look so damn good. Thanks also to the following people: my mum for being all hands on deck during the write-up; the Boss family for their pad; all the peeps who visited us from far away during our six years in Hong Kong; our friends who helped make Happy Valley and beyond home; Tessy for being part of our family; Foosle, for being there for me always; Benji, Mima and Rupie for the family fun times; and Digby and Etienne, who joined the party along the way. Lastly, thanks to Pipster, my husband and best friend who made the whole weird and wonderful Hong Kong journey possible.

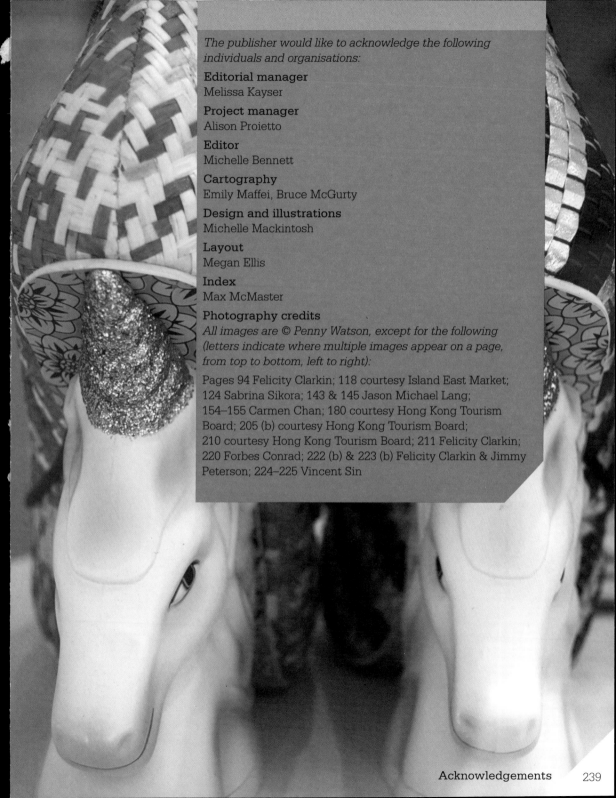

The publisher would like to acknowledge the following individuals and organisations:

Editorial manager
Melissa Kayser

Project manager
Alison Proietto

Editor
Michelle Bennett

Cartography
Emily Maffei, Bruce McGurty

Design and illustrations
Michelle Mackintosh

Layout
Megan Ellis

Index
Max McMaster

Photography credits
All images are © Penny Watson, except for the following (letters indicate where multiple images appear on a page, from top to bottom, left to right):

Pages 94 Felicity Clarkin; 118 courtesy Island East Market; 124 Sabrina Sikora; 143 & 145 Jason Michael Lang; 154–155 Carmen Chan; 180 courtesy Hong Kong Tourism Board; 205 (b) courtesy Hong Kong Tourism Board; 210 courtesy Hong Kong Tourism Board; 211 Felicity Clarkin; 220 Forbes Conrad; 222 (b) & 223 (b) Felicity Clarkin & Jimmy Peterson; 224–225 Vincent Sin

Explore Australia Publishing Pty Ltd
Ground Floor, Building 1, 658 Church Street,
Richmond, VIC 3121

Explore Australia Publishing Pty Ltd is a division of Hardie Grant Publishing Pty Ltd

hardie grant publishing

Published by Explore Australia Publishing Pty Ltd, 2015

A Cataloguing-in-Publication entry is available from the catalogue of the National
Library of Australia at www.nla.gov.au

The maps in this publication incorporate data © OpenStreetMap contributors.
OpenStreetMap is made available under the Open Database License:
http://opendatacommons.org/licenses/odbl/1.0/.
Any rights in individual contents of the database are licensed under the
Database Contents License: http://opendatacommons.org/licenses/dbcl/1.0/
See more at: http://opendatacommons.org/licenses/odbl/

Disclaimer
The Database is licensed by the Licensor 'as is' and without any warranty of any
kind, either express, implied, or arising by statute, custom, course of dealing, or trade
usage. Licensor specifically disclaims any and all implied warranties or conditions
of title, non-infringement, accuracy or completeness, the presence or absence of
errors, fitness for a particular purpose, merchantability, or otherwise. While every
care is taken to ensure the accuracy of the data within this product, the owners of
the data do not make any representations or warranties about its accuracy, reliability,
completeness or suitability for any particular purpose and, to the extent permitted
by law, the owners of the data disclaim all responsibility and all liability (including
without limitation, liability in negligence) for all expenses, losses, damages,
(including indirect or consequential damages) and costs which might be incurred as
a result of the data being inaccurate or incomplete in any way and for any reason.

ISBN-13 9781741174694

10 9 8 7 6 5 4 3 2 1

Printed and bound in China by 1010 Printing International Ltd

Publisher's note: Every effort has been made to ensure that the information in this
book is accurate at the time of going to press. The publisher welcomes information
and suggestions for correction or improvement. Email: info@exploreaustralia.net.au

Publisher's disclaimer: The publisher cannot accept responsibility for any errors or
omissions. The representation on the maps of any road or track is not necessarily
evidence of public right of way. The publisher cannot be held responsible for any
injury, loss or damage incurred during travel. It is vital to research any proposed
trip thoroughly and seek the advice of relevant government bodies and travel
organisations before you leave.